"If You Can't Stand the Heat, Get Out of the Kitchen!"

VOLUME II

Harry Truman

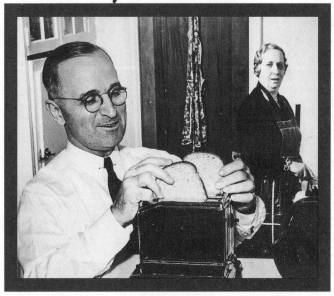

Junior Service League
Independence, Missouri

If You Can't Stand the Heat, Get Out of the Kitchen!"

VOLUME II

Copyright © 1999
The Independence Junior Service League
P.O. Box 1571
Independence, MO 64055

Library of Congress Number: 98-075370
ISBN: 0-9615328-2-3

Designed, Edited, and Manufactured by
Favorite Recipes® Press
an imprint of

P.O. Box 305142
Nashville, Tennessee 37230
1-800-358-0560

Book Design: Starletta Polster
Art Director: Steve Newman
Project Manager: Susan Larson

Manufactured in the United States of America
First Printing: 1999   10,000 copies

Table of Contents

Introduction

A well-turned phrase bears repeating. Thus it is used to name the revision of the Independence, Missouri, Junior Service League's cookbook "If You Can't Stand the Heat, Get Out of the Kitchen!"

President Harry S. Truman's terse, widely quoted words are a fitting commentary on both his personal life and his political one, reflecting his strong and simple Midwestern values. Bess shared his outlook, and in speeches and comments, Harry Truman often gave metaphorical meaning to this famous quotation in homey judgments on life, family, and conduct. Equally so, this revised cookbook is a fitting commentary on our changing lifestyles. It updates recipes and features economy of ingredients, diversity in culinary tastes, and efficiency in food preparation.

President Truman often said his favorite meal was "meat and potatoes." But in 1911 while courting Bess, who was an excellent cook, he wrote a kind note to her saying, "That cake couldn't be beat." A week later he wrote, "That stew couldn't be beat." And soon exclaimed, "There is nothing better than cake but more cake and the same goes for pie." He won over that young lady in marriage in 1919— or perhaps it was the other way around!

Even as president, Harry Truman requested simpler and tastier meals from the White House staff. Yet he was so delighted with his first birthday cake prepared by the head White House cook, he made his way to the kitchen to thank her. According to the chief butler, it was the first time a president had been in the White House kitchen since Coolidge!

In making these few remarks for this recipe collection and its Truman association, I also thank the ladies of the Independence Junior Service League for the unstinting support and many services they generously gave to the Truman Library over the quarter of a century I was there.

— Ben Zobrist
Former Director
Harry S. Truman Library

★ ★ ★ ★ ★

THE INDEPENDENCE JUNIOR SERVICE LEAGUE

Junior Service League of Independence trains volunteers for leadership and initiates service in response to community needs while offering opportunities for personal growth to women.

The purpose of this organization shall be to arouse interest among its members in the social, economic, educational, cultural, and civic conditions of their community and to prepare them for intelligent participation in activities of value to the community.

For over 50 years, the women of Junior Service League have provided volunteer service and financial assistance to many worthwhile projects in Eastern Jackson County. A sampling of the projects supported in the past include: Kids on the Block (a puppet show about disabilities, presented to all local elementary schools); youth mentoring; The Bess Wallace Truman Award; Hope House; Child Abuse Prevention Association (CAPA); Work Express; Truman Depot Restoration Project; and the Truman Heartland Arts Alliance.

Junior Service League looks for projects that will enhance the quality of life for citizens of Eastern Jackson County and tries to assist in completing those efforts.

★ ★ ★ ★ ★

★ ★ ★ ★ ★

Expectations

GREAT STARTS & LIBATIONS

*"I am the hired man of one hundred and fifty million
people, and it is a job that keeps me right busy."*

★ ★ ★ ★ ★

"Truman is honest and patriotic and has a head full of good horse sense. Besides, he has guts." And so the assessment of the 33rd President of the United States, Harry S. Truman, began. Little did John Nance Garner realize when he penned those words in 1945 how they would prove to capture the essence of a great man with whom present-day leaders of both political parties seek to ally themselves.

The tumultuous days and wrenching decisions made during the presidency of Harry S. Truman are well documented and widely recognized. We still feel the effects in current international politics of the decision to drop the A-bomb, the birth of the United Nations, the Truman Doctrine, the Marshall Plan, and the formation of NATO, to name only a few.

Truman's legacy is indisputable. Seemingly endless accounts and analyses of his administration and life are readily available. Because this is primarily a cookbook and not a history book, we do not presume to bring a scholarly look at Harry Truman. Rather, we hope to offer a few interesting facts and anecdotes to you that provide a glimpse into the gentle humanity and wit of Independence's favorite son.

What a Ball

8 ounces cream cheese, softened
3 ounces bleu cheese, crumbled
¼ cup margarine

1 tablespoon sherry
½ cup raisins
½ cup chopped pecans

Combine the cream cheese, blue cheese, margarine, sherry and raisins in a bowl and mix well.

Shape into a ball. Roll in the pecans in a shallow dish to coat. Cover with plastic wrap and refrigerate until ready to serve.

Variation: May add ½ cup chopped pecans to the cream cheese mixture.

Yield: 12 servings

Sunflower Cheese Ball

1½ cups lightly salted roasted
**   sunflower kernels**
8 ounces cream cheese, softened
3 ounces bleu cheese, crumbled
¼ cup finely chopped celery
¼ cup finely chopped green
**   onions**

2 tablespoons sour cream
1 teaspoon instant chicken
**   bouillon granules**
⅛ teaspoon ground red pepper
1 (15-ounce) package nacho
**   cheese tortilla chips**

Combine 1 cup of the sunflower kernels, cream cheese, blue cheese, celery, green onions, sour cream, bouillon granules and red pepper in a bowl and mix well.

Shape into a ball. Roll in the remaining ½ cup of sunflower kernels in a shallow dish to coat. Wrap in plastic wrap. Refrigerate for 8 or more hours.

Let stand at room temperature for 20 to 30 minutes or until softened. Press the tortilla chips into the side of the cheese ball to resemble flower petals. Serve with the remaining chips.

Yield: 12 servings

Smoky Salmon Ball

1 (16-ounce) can pink salmon,
* drained*
8 ounces cream cheese, softened
1 tablespoon lemon juice

2 teaspoons prepared horseradish
¼ teaspoon liquid smoke
½ cup chopped pecans
¼ cup chopped parsley

Flake the salmon. Remove the skin and bones.

Combine the salmon, cream cheese, lemon juice, horseradish and liquid smoke in a bowl and mix well. Cover with plastic wrap. Chill for several hours.

Combine the pecans and parsley in a shallow dish and mix well. Shape the salmon mixture into a ball or log. Roll in the pecan mixture to coat. Serve with crackers.

Yield: 16 servings

Great Balls of Shrimp

8 ounces cream cheese, softened
1 (7-ounce) can tiny shrimp,
* drained*
1 teaspoon minced dried onion

1 teaspoon lemon juice
1½ teaspoons prepared mustard
Salt and pepper to taste
1 cup crushed cornflakes

Combine the cream cheese, shrimp, onion, lemon juice, mustard, salt and pepper in a bowl and mix well.

Shape into 16 balls. Roll in the cornflakes in a shallow dish to coat. Chill, covered, for 1 to 2 hours.

Yield: 12 servings

Baked Goat Cheese

½ teaspoon minced garlic
8 ounces goat cheese, chopped
½ cup chopped fresh basil leaves

4 ounces oil-packed sun-dried
   tomatoes, chopped

Sprinkle the garlic over the bottom of a small baking dish coated with olive oil. Sprinkle the goat cheese over the garlic.

Bake at 450 degrees for 25 minutes or until the cheese is very soft and bubbly.

Stir in the basil and sun-dried tomatoes. Place in a serving dish. Garnish with pine nuts. Serve with Italian crostini or crisp crackers.

Yield: 4 servings

Country Fare

1 (12-ounce) package bacon
16 ounces extra sharp Cheddar
   cheese, shredded
1 bunch green onions, chopped

2 cups mayonnaise
1 teaspoon cayenne
½ cup slivered almonds, toasted

Cook the bacon in a skillet until crisp; drain. Crumble the bacon.

Combine the bacon, cheese, green onions, mayonnaise and cayenne in a bowl and mix well.

Sprinkle the almonds in the bottom of an oiled 7-cup ring mold. Press the cheese mixture in the mold. Chill, covered, for several hours.

Unmold the cheese ring onto a serving platter. Place a small custard cup filled with strawberry preserves in the center of the ring. Serve with crackers or French bread slices.

Yield: 20 servings

Double-Up Black Bean Dip

1 (15-ounce) can black beans,
    rinsed, drained
1 teaspoon vegetable oil
½ cup chopped onion
2 cloves of garlic, minced
⅔ cup picante sauce

½ teaspoon ground cumin
½ teaspoon chili powder
¼ cup shredded Monterey Jack
    cheese
1 tablespoon lime juice

Pour the beans into a bowl. Mash with a fork until chunky or of the desired consistency. Set aside.

Heat the oil in a nonstick skillet over medium heat. Sauté the onion and garlic in the oil until tender. Add the beans, picante sauce, cumin and chili powder and mix well.

Cook for 5 minutes or until of the desired consistency, stirring constantly. Remove from heat.

Add the cheese and lime juice and mix well.

Variation: May be served warm or at room temperature with tortilla chips.

Yield: 16 servings

Black Bean Salsa

2 medium tomatoes
1 red bell pepper
1 green bell pepper
1 (15-ounce) can black beans, rinsed, drained
1½ cups cooked fresh corn kernels
½ cup finely chopped red onion
1 or 2 fresh green serrano peppers, thinly sliced
⅓ cup fresh lime juice
⅓ cup olive oil
⅓ cup chopped fresh cilantro
1 teaspoon salt
½ teaspoon ground cumin
Pinch of cayenne

Chop the tomatoes, red bell pepper and green bell pepper into ¼-inch pieces.

Combine the tomatoes, red bell pepper, green bell pepper, black beans, corn, onion, serrano peppers, lime juice, olive oil, cilantro, salt, cumin, and cayenne in a large bowl and mix well.

Chill, covered, for several hours. Bring to room temperature before serving.

Variation: May substitute jalapeños for the serrano peppers.

Yield: 15 servings

Gemini Crab Meat Dip

8 ounces cream cheese
¼ cup mayonnaise
1 clove of garlic, minced
1 teaspoon grated onion
1 teaspoon dry mustard
1 teaspoon sugar
3 tablespoons white wine
1 (4-ounce) can crab meat

Melt the cream cheese in a saucepan over low heat.

Add the mayonnaise and mix well. Add the garlic, onion, mustard and sugar and mix well. Add the wine and crab meat and mix well.

Yield: 12 servings

Island Salsa

1 (8-ounce) can crushed
    pineapple, drained
¼ cup chopped fresh cilantro
2 to 3 cloves of garlic, minced

1 jalapeño, seeded, chopped
2 tablespoons lime juice
½ teaspoon salt

Combine the pineapple, cilantro, garlic, jalapeño, lime juice and salt in a bowl and mix well.

Chill, covered, for 2 or more hours.

Yield: 4 servings

Jackson County Caviar

2 (4-ounce) cans chopped black
    olives
2 (4-ounce) cans chopped green
    chiles
2 tomatoes, peeled, chopped
3 green onions, chopped

1 tablespoon olive oil
2 cloves of garlic, minced
2 teaspoons red wine vinegar
1 teaspoon pepper
⅛ teaspoon seasoned salt

Combine the olives, chiles, tomatoes, green onions, olive oil, garlic, vinegar, pepper and seasoned salt in a bowl and mix well.

Chill, covered, for several hours. Serve with chips.

Yield: 12 servings

Loaded Spinach Dip

1 (10-ounce) package frozen
   chopped spinach, thawed,
   drained
½ (10-ounce) jar Alfredo sauce
1 clove of garlic, minced
Pepper to taste
1 cup grated Parmesan cheese

1 cup shredded mozzarella cheese
4 ounces Velveeta cheese
1 cup sour cream
4 ounces cream cheese, softened
½ (15-ounce) can tomatoes
½ (14-ounce) can chopped
   artichokes

Combine the spinach, Alfredo sauce, garlic, pepper, Parmesan cheese, mozzarella cheese, Velveeta cheese, sour cream, cream cheese, tomatoes and artichokes in a food processor container. Pulse until well mixed. Pour into a microwave-safe dish.

Microwave until cheeses are melted, stirring every 2 minutes.

Yield: 16 servings

Reuben Dip

3 ounces cream cheese
⅓ cup sour cream
½ cup shredded Swiss cheese
4 ounces corned beef, chopped

⅓ cup sauerkraut, drained
½ teaspoon Worcestershire sauce
2 tablespoons milk

Combine the cream cheese, sour cream, Swiss cheese, corned beef, sauerkraut, Worcestershire sauce and milk in a saucepan.

Cook over low heat until cheeses are melted, stirring occasionally; add additional milk to thin if desired. Serve with bagel chips.

Yield: 8 servings

Toasted Almond Party Spread

8 ounces cream cheese, softened
1½ cups shredded Swiss cheese
⅓ cup mayonnaise-style salad
 dressing
2 tablespoons chopped green
 onion

⅛ teaspoon pepper
⅛ teaspoon ground nutmeg
⅓ cup sliced almonds,
 toasted

Combine the cream cheese, Swiss cheese, salad dressing, green onion, pepper, nutmeg and ⅓ cup almonds in a bowl and mix well. Spread in a 9-inch pie or quiche dish.

Bake in a preheated 350-degree oven for 15 minutes. Garnish with additional toasted almonds. Serve with assorted crackers or toasted bread.

Yield: 10 servings

"I used to watch my father and mother closely
to learn what I could do to please them,
just as I did with my schoolteachers and playmates.
Because of my efforts to get along with my associates
I usually was able to get what I wanted."

Gouda Cheese Bundles

**1 (7-ounce) round of Gouda
  cheese
1 (8-count) can crescent rolls**

**1 to 2 tablespoons Dijon mustard
1 egg, lightly beaten**

Remove the wax from the cheese. Unroll the crescent dough on a greased baking sheet.

Spread enough mustard to lightly coat the dough, or to taste. Place the cheese in the center of the coated dough. Bring the corners of the dough to the center. Pinch together to enclose the cheese. Brush with the egg.

Bake at 350 degrees for 20 minutes. Serve with sliced apples and pears.

Yield: 8 servings

Wrapped Asparagus

**36 asparagus spears
36 (4-inch-long) slices prosciutto
4 ounces bleu cheese, crumbled
½ cup olive oil
½ cup vegetable oil**

**½ cup balsamic vinegar
½ teaspoon salt
½ teaspoon pepper
½ teaspoon basil**

Trim the asparagus spears 4 to 6 inches long. Peel the ends.

Place the asparagus spears in a microwave-safe dish. Pour ½ cup water over the asparagus. Cover with plastic wrap. Microwave on High for 2½ to 3 minutes or until tender-crisp; drain.

Plunge the blanched asparagus into ice water in a bowl; drain.

Wrap each asparagus spear with 1 slice of prosciutto. Arrange on a serving platter. Sprinkle the bleu cheese over the prosciutto-wrapped asparagus.

Combine the olive oil, vegetable oil, vinegar, salt, pepper and basil in a bowl and mix well. Pour over the bleu cheese.

Yield: 10 servings

 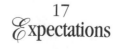

Crescent Veggie Appetizers

2 (8-count) cans crescent rolls
8 ounces cream cheese, softened
½ cup sour cream
1 teaspoon dried dillweed
⅛ teaspoon garlic powder
½ cup finely chopped green bell
   pepper

½ cup finely chopped red bell
   pepper
½ cup finely chopped broccoli
½ cup finely chopped carrot
½ cup finely chopped cucumber
½ cup finely chopped green
   onions

Remove dough from cans in rolled sections, 2 sections from each can. Cut each section into 8 slices. Place slices, cut side down, on ungreased baking sheets.

Bake in a preheated 375-degree oven for 11 to 13 minutes or until golden brown. Cool for 1 minute. Loosen with a spatula and slide onto a wire rack to cool.

Combine the cream cheese, sour cream, dillweed and garlic powder in a bowl and mix until smooth. Spread over the crescent slices. Sprinkle with the vegetables.

Variation: May substitute 3 cups finely chopped vegetables of choice for the green bell pepper, red bell pepper, broccoli, carrot, cucumber and green onions.

Yield: 16 servings

Whistle Stop Wings

5 pounds chicken wings
2 cups flour
Vegetable oil for deep frying
½ cup soy sauce

½ cup sugar
½ teaspoon garlic powder
⅓ cup sesame seeds

Coat the chicken with flour, shaking off excess.

Pour the oil ¾- to 1-inch deep into a large skillet and heat. Add the chicken. Cook for 14 minutes or until cooked through and golden brown, turning once; drain.

Combine the soy sauce, sugar and garlic powder in a saucepan and mix well. Bring to a boil, stirring constantly. Remove from heat.

Dip the chicken in the soy sauce mixture, coating completely. Drain on paper towels. Sprinkle with the sesame seeds.

Variation: May substitute chicken thighs for the chicken wings.

Yield: 16 servings

Amaretto Lemon Freeze

1 (46-ounce) can pineapple juice
3 cups amaretto
1 (12-ounce) can frozen pink
   lemonade concentrate, thawed
1 (6-ounce) can frozen pink
   lemonade concentrate, thawed

⅓ cup lemon juice
1 (3-liter) bottle lemon-lime
   soda, chilled

Combine the pineapple juice, amaretto, pink lemonade concentrate and lemon juice in a large plastic container and mix well.

Freeze, covered, for 8 or more hours, stirring twice.

Combine equal portions of the frozen mixture and lemon-lime soda in a cup and mix well. Serve immediately.

Yield: 48 (½-cup) servings

Cappuccino Mix

1 cup coffee creamer
1 cup instant chocolate milk mix
⅔ cup instant coffee

½ cup confectioners' sugar
½ teaspoon cinnamon

Combine the coffee creamer, chocolate milk mix, instant coffee, confectioners' sugar and cinnamon in a bowl and mix well.

Stir 1 tablespoon of coffee creamer mixture into 1 cup of hot water and mix well.

Store remaining mixture in an airtight container.

Yield: 20 servings

Best-Kept-Secret Margaritas

1 (12-ounce) can frozen limeade concentrate, thawed
1 (12-ounce) bottle light beer

12 ounces tequila
2 to 4 cups ice
2 limes

Combine the limeade concentrate, beer, tequila and ice in a blender container. Pulse until slushy.

Pour ¼ cup salt into a shallow dish. Cut the limes into slices. Rub a lime slice on the rim of a glass. Dip the rim of the glass into the salt. Repeat with the remaining lime slices and glasses.

Fill glasses with tequila mixture. Garnish with lime slices.

Yield: 4 servings

Frozen Margaritas

6 (6-ounce) cans frozen limeade concentrate, thawed
1 fifth light tequila

1¼ cups Triple Sec
9 cups water

Combine the limeade concentrate, tequila, Triple Sec and water in a large plastic container and mix well. Freeze, covered, for 2 days.

Yield: 36 (½-cup) servings

Peach Fuzz

**1 (6-ounce) can frozen limeade
concentrate
6 ounces vodka**

**3 fresh peaches, sliced
12 ice cubes**

Combine the limeade concentrate, vodka, peaches and ice cubes in a blender container and process until well blended.

Freeze, covered, for several hours.

Yield: 12 servings

Piña Colada Slush

**1 (46-ounce) can pineapple juice
2 (12-ounce) cans frozen
lemonade concentrate, thawed
3 cups water
2 cups light rum**

**1 (15-ounce) can cream of
coconut
1 (3-liter) bottle lemon-lime
soda, chilled**

Combine the pineapple juice, lemonade concentrate, water, rum and cream of coconut in a large plastic container and mix well.

Freeze, covered, for 8 or more hours, stirring twice.

Combine equal portions of the frozen mixture and lemon-lime soda in a cup and mix well. Serve immediately.

Yield: 48 (½-cup) servings

LIGHTER FARE

*"Criticism is something (a president) gets every day,
just like breakfast."*

Harry S. Truman was born in Lamar, Missouri, in 1884. His parents John and Martha Truman could not decide whether his middle name should honor his or her father (Solomon or Shipp), so they compromised with the letter S, formally giving young Harry neither name. When he was six years old, the family moved to Independence, Missouri.

As a boy, Harry had an upbringing typical of thousands across the United States: daily chores, school, games, picnics, and piano lessons. Harry was an avid student and by eight or nine years old was reading "everything I could get my hands on — histories and encyclopedias and everything else." He had read the Bible through twice before his twelfth birthday. He remained an avid reader his entire life — he read five newspapers a day, even in his retirement.

During grade school and high school, Harry took piano lessons. His mother had planned for him to be a concert pianist, and he practiced an hour each day at 5:00 a.m. After high school graduation, because of family finances, he could not pursue higher education and his formal music training ended also. But Harry's love for music was an integral part of his life, and he was frequently asked to play, even as president. Many people assume the "Missouri Waltz" was a favored piece, but Harry said "…the Missouri Waltz may be a good piece of popular music, but in my opinion it is not a proper state song." Harry was more fond of classical music, particularly Chopin. In 1952, Harry played Mozart on the White House piano for 30 million television viewers as he gave them a tour of the renovated Executive Mansion.

Cream of Brie and Red Pepper Soup

½ cup minced leeks
4 tablespoons butter
3 tablespoons flour
5¼ cups hot chicken stock
20 ounces brie, rinds discarded, cut into pieces

1¼ cups cream
Salt and pepper to taste
1 pound red bell peppers, cored, seeded
2 tablespoons sweet paprika

Cook the leeks in 2 tablespoons of the butter in a saucepan until translucent. Stir in 2 tablespoons of the flour.

Cook for 2 minutes, stirring constantly. Whisk in 4 cups of the stock. Simmer until reduced to 2¼ cups.

Add the brie. Cook until brie is melted, stirring constantly. Stir in ¼ cup of the cream, salt and pepper. Remove from heat.

Steam the bell peppers in a steamer until the skins pull away; drain. Peel the peppers and chop finely. Cook the peppers for 1 minute in the remaining 2 tablespoons butter in a saucepan.

Stir in the paprika and the remaining 1 tablespoon flour. Cook for 2 minutes, stirring constantly.

Cover and continue cooking until the bell peppers are tender. Stir in the remaining 1¼ cups stock and the remaining 1 cup cream. Simmer until reduced to 3 cups, stirring occasionally.

Purée in a food processor. Season with salt and pepper.

Fill a soup ladle with the red pepper mixture. Fill another soup ladle with the brie mixture. Pour at the same time into a warmed soup bowl. Swirl together with a toothpick or wooden skewer. Garnish with sour cream and chives. Repeat with remaining bowls.

Variation: May substitute shallots for the leeks and half-and-half for the cream.

Yield: 6 servings

Cheesy Clam Chowder

2 tablespoons chopped onion
2 tablespoons butter
1 (10-ounce) can cheese soup
5 ounces milk

1 (16-ounce) can tomatoes
1 (7-ounce) can minced clams
1 tablespoon parsley
Pepper to taste

Cook the onion in the butter in a saucepan until golden.

Add the cheese soup and milk and mix well. Add the tomatoes, clams, parsley and pepper and mix well.

Cook until heated through, stirring occasionally.

Yield: 4 servings

 # First Edition Lentil Soup

1 (16-ounce) package lentils,
    rinsed, drained
2 or 3 bay leaves
Salt and pepper to taste
2 beef bouillon cubes
8 ounces carrots, sliced
½ large onion, chopped

2 large potatoes, chopped
2 teaspoons Worcestershire sauce
4 or 5 bacon slices, cut into
    1-inch pieces
1 pound Polish sausage, skin
    removed, sliced

Combine the lentils, bay leaves, salt, pepper and 6 cups cold water in a large saucepan. Bring to a boil. Reduce the heat. Add the bouillon cubes, carrots, onion, potatoes, Worcestershire sauce and bacon.

Cook for 30 minutes. Add the Polish sausage. Cook for 30 minutes. Ladle into individual bowls and sprinkle each with wine vinegar.

Yield: 8 servings

Gazpacho

8 ripe tomatoes
3 cucumbers
8 cloves of garlic
1 large yellow onion
1 zucchini
3 red, yellow or green bell
    peppers

⅔ cup olive oil
¼ cup red wine vinegar
2 cups tomato juice
Salt and pepper to taste

Seed and chop the tomatoes. Place in a large bowl. Peel, seed and chop the cucumbers. Add to the tomatoes. Mince the garlic. Add to the tomatoes.

Peel the yellow onion and slice into thirds. Cut the zucchini into halves horizontally. Brush the onion, zucchini and bell peppers with the olive oil. Place on a baking sheet.

Broil until zucchini and onions are roasted and bell peppers are blistered and black. Cool completely.

Cut the bell peppers into halves. Remove the seeds and membranes. Chop the bell peppers, zucchini and onion coarsely.

Purée the bell peppers, zucchini and onion in a food processor. Add the puréed mixture to the tomato mixture. Add the vinegar and tomato juice and mix well. Stir in the remaining olive oil, salt and pepper.

Chill, covered, for 2 or more hours. Garnish with thinly sliced scallions and chopped red onion.

Yield: 6 servings

Lasagna Soup

1 pound ground beef
1 medium onion, chopped
2 cloves of garlic, minced
4 cups water
2 (14½-ounce) cans diced tomatoes in olive oil, garlic and spices
6 ounces tomato paste

4 ounces miniature lasagna noodles, uncooked
1 tablespoon brown sugar
½ teaspoon Italian seasoning
¼ teaspoon pepper
1½ cups Italian-style croutons
½ cup shredded mozzarella cheese

Brown the ground beef with the onion and garlic in a skillet, stirring until the ground beef is crumbly; drain.

Stir in the water, tomatoes and tomato paste. Add the lasagna noodles, brown sugar, Italian seasoning and pepper and mix well.

Bring to a boil. Simmer, covered, for 10 minutes. Preheat the broiler.

Pour the soup into 6 ovenproof soup bowls. Top each with ¼ cup croutons. Sprinkle with cheese.

Broil 3 to 4 inches from the heat source for 1 to 2 minutes or until the cheese is melted.

Variation: May substitute sausage for the ground beef.

Yield: 6 servings

Pot of Gold Soup

2 tablespoons butter
1 medium onion, chopped
1 pound carrots, thinly sliced
5 cups chicken stock

1 cup orange juice
1 cup cream
Nutmeg to taste
Salt and pepper to taste

Melt the butter in a large saucepan. Add the onion and carrots. Cook, covered, over low heat for 5 to 7 minutes. Pour in the stock.

Bring to a boil. Simmer until carrots are tender-crisp.

Purée in a food processor. Return to the saucepan. Stir in the orange juice, cream, nutmeg, salt and pepper.

Cook until heated through; do not boil. Garnish with parsley or chives.

Yield: 4 servings

Three Trails Cheese Soup

½ cup margarine
1 cup minced carrots
1 cup chopped onion
1 cup chopped celery

½ cup flour
3 cups chicken broth
3 cups half-and-half
2 cups chopped Velveeta

Melt the margarine in a large skillet. Add the carrots, onion and celery. Sauté the vegetables until tender-crisp. Stir in the flour.

Cook on medium-high heat until the flour is light brown. Whisk in the broth gradually.

Cook until of the desired consistency. Stir in the half-and-half; do not boil. Add the cheese.

Cook until the cheese is melted, stirring constantly.

Ladle into soup bowls. Garnish with fresh parsley.

Yield: 6 servings

ABC Sandwiches

1 bunch asparagus, trimmed
12 slices bread

1 pound bacon, crisp-fried
6 slices Cheddar cheese

Steam the asparagus in a steamer until tender-crisp; drain.

Toast the bread.

Layer the asparagus, bacon and Cheddar cheese evenly on 6 slices of toast. Top with the remaining toast. Place on a microwave-safe plate.

Microwave on High for 1 minute or until the cheese melts.

Yield: 6 sandwiches

Grilled Bacon, Cheese and Tomato Sandwiches

¼ cup butter or margarine,
**   softened**
8 slices ½-inch-thick French
**   bread**

8 (1-ounce) slices Swiss cheese
3 plum tomatoes, thinly sliced
½ teaspoon dried basil
12 slices bacon, crisp-fried

Spread the butter on one side of each bread slice.

Layer the cheese, tomatoes, basil and bacon evenly over 4 slices of the bread, buttered side down. Top with the remaining bread, buttered side up.

Grill in a skillet until golden on both sides, turning once.

Yield: 4 servings

MJC Executive Croissant Sandwiches

2 Bartlett pears
1 teaspoon lemon juice
1/4 cup water
6 (2½-ounce) butter croissants
Curry Sauce with Capers
18 ounces smoked turkey,
    thinly sliced

6 ounces mixed spring greens
1 large red onion, thinly sliced
6 (1-ounce) slices Provolone
    cheese

Slice the pears thinly. Combine the lemon juice and water in a large bowl. Add the pears and toss to coat; drain.

Cut the croissants into halves. Spread the curry sauce evenly over each half. Layer the turkey, mixed spring greens, onion and cheese evenly over the 6 bottom halves of the croissants.

Arrange the pear slices in a fan shape over the layers. Top with the 6 top halves of the croissants.

Curry Sauce with Capers

1/2 cup mayonnaise
1/4 cup sour cream
1/2 teaspoon chopped dried herbs
1/8 teaspoon salt
3/8 teaspoon curry powder
1 tablespoon minced dried onion

1/2 tablespoon chopped fresh
    parsley
1 teaspoon lemon juice
1 tablespoon capers, drained
1/4 teaspoon Worcestershire sauce

Combine the mayonnaise, sour cream, herbs, salt, curry powder, onion, parsley, lemon juice, capers and Worcestershire sauce in a bowl and mix well.

Chill, covered, for 8 to 12 hours.

Yield: 6 servings

Sweet Smoky Sandwiches

2 Granny Smith apples
2 tablespoons lemon juice
½ cup cream cheese with honey
*   and nuts, softened*

8 slices wheat berry bread
12 ounces deli smoked turkey,
*   thinly sliced*

Rinse and pat the apples dry. Cut into thin slices.

Combine the apple slices and lemon juice in a bowl and toss the slices to coat. Drain the apple slices.

Spread the cream cheese evenly over the 8 slices of bread.

Layer the turkey and apple slices evenly over the cream cheese on 4 bread slices.

Top with the 4 remaining bread slices, cream cheese side down.

Yield: 4 servings

"I have never fussed too much about food. I eat
what I like and pass up what I do not. I never complain.
When I was in the army, as commanding officer of a battery,
one of my staff kicked about the food. I put him in
the kitchen to take charge and see what he could do.
I think that is the proper way to deal with critics."

Chocolate Zucchini Bread

2⅓ *cups flour*
2 *cups sugar*
½ *cup unsweetened cocoa*
2 *teaspoons salt*
1 *teaspoon cinnamon*
2 *teaspoons baking soda*

¼ *teaspoon baking powder*
3 *eggs*
1 *cup vegetable oil*
2 *teaspoons vanilla extract*
3 *cups shredded zucchini*
½ *cup pecan pieces*

Combine the flour, sugar, cocoa, salt, cinnamon, baking soda and baking powder in a bowl and mix well.

Beat the eggs, oil and vanilla in a mixer bowl. Stir in the zucchini.

Add the dry ingredients and mix well. Stir in the pecans. Pour the batter into 2 greased loaf pans.

Bake in a preheated 350-degree oven for 45 to 55 minutes or until the loaves test done. Cool in the pans for 10 minutes. Remove to a wire rack to cool completely.

Yield: 24 slices

Brookside Stromboli

1 (1-pound) loaf frozen bread
   dough, thawed
2 egg yolks
1 tablespoon grated Parmesan
   cheese
1 teaspoon minced parsley
1½ teaspoons garlic powder

1 teaspoon oregano
¼ teaspoon pepper
2 tablespoons vegetable oil
8 ounces pepperoni, thinly sliced
10 ounces Cheddar cheese,
   shredded
2 egg whites

Roll the bread dough into a rectangle on a lightly floured surface.

Combine the egg yolks, Parmesan cheese, parsley, garlic powder, oregano, pepper and oil in a bowl and mix well. Spread over the dough.

Arrange the pepperoni slices over the egg yolk mixture. Sprinkle the Cheddar cheese over the pepperoni.

Roll as for a jelly roll, sealing the edge and ends. Place seam side down on a greased baking sheet. Brush with egg whites.

Bake at 350 degrees for 30 to 40 minutes or until golden brown.

Yield: 6 servings

Dilly Bread

1 envelope active dry yeast
½ cup lukewarm water
1 cup creamed cottage cheese
1 tablespoon butter
1 egg
2 tablespoons chopped onion
2 tablespoons dillseeds

2 tablespoons sugar
1 teaspoon salt
¼ teaspoon baking soda
2½ cups flour
2 tablespoons butter, softened
Salt to taste

Dissolve the yeast in ½ cup lukewarm water.

Combine the cottage cheese, 1 tablespoon butter, egg, onion, dillseeds, sugar, 1 teaspoon salt, baking soda and dissolved yeast in a mixer bowl and beat at medium-high speed. Stir in the flour, gradually, to make a stiff dough.

Place the dough in a greased bowl, turning to coat the surface. Let rise, covered, in a warm place until doubled in bulk, about 1 hour.

Punch the dough down. Place in a greased 8-inch round baking dish. Let rise for 35 minutes or until doubled in bulk.

Bake at 350 degrees for 40 to 50 minutes or until golden brown. Brush with 2 tablespoons butter. Sprinkle generously with salt. Serve immediately.

Yield: 9 servings

Orange Cranberry Bread

1 cup sugar
2 cups flour
½ teaspoon baking powder
½ teaspoon salt
½ teaspoon baking soda
1 egg
2 tablespoons melted margarine

2 tablespoons hot water
½ cup orange juice
1 tablespoon grated orange peel
1 cup fresh cranberries, chopped
½ cup chopped walnuts or
  pecans

Combine the sugar, flour, baking powder, salt and baking soda in a bowl and mix well.

Beat the egg, margarine, water, orange juice and orange peel in a bowl.

Add the orange juice mixture to the dry ingredients. Stir just until mixed.

Stir in the cranberries and walnuts. Spoon into a greased and floured loaf pan.

Bake at 350 degrees for 1 hour or until the loaf tests done. Cool in the pan for 10 minutes. Remove to a wire rack to cool completely.

Yield: 12 servings

Sunrise Muffins

1 pound bacon
1 cup milk
1 cup pancake syrup
2 eggs
¾ cup wheat flour
¾ cup all-purpose flour

½ cup firmly packed brown sugar
½ teaspoon salt
2 teaspoons baking powder
1 teaspoon baking soda
1 cup rolled oats

Cook the bacon in a skillet until crisp; drain. Crumble into small pieces.

Combine the milk, syrup, and eggs in a large bowl and mix well.

Combine the wheat flour, all-purpose flour, brown sugar, salt, baking powder, baking soda and oats in a bowl and mix well. Add to the milk mixture and mix well. Stir in the crumbled bacon.

Fill 18 greased muffin cups ⅔ full.

Bake at 350 degrees for 15 to 18 minutes or until a wooden pick inserted in the center of the muffins comes out clean.

Variation: May substitute miniature muffin pans for regular muffin pans and adjust the cooking time to 13 to 15 minutes, or use large muffin pans and bake for 20 to 25 minutes.

Yield: 18 muffins

Blanketed Grapefruit Wedges

2 large grapefruit
1 (3-ounce) package lemon
  gelatin
1 cup sugar
1 teaspoon honey

Juice of 1 lemon
1 (3-ounce) package cream
  cheese, softened
1 cup whipping cream, whipped

Cut the grapefruit into halves. Remove the sections, reserving the shells and juice.

Combine the gelatin and sugar in a bowl.

Add enough water to the reserved juice to make 2 cups. Bring the liquid to a boil in a saucepan. Pour over the gelatin and sugar and stir until dissolved. Chill until partially set. Stir in the grapefruit sections. Pour into the reserved shells. Chill until set.

Combine the honey, lemon and cream cheese in a mixer bowl; mix well. Fold in the whipped cream.

Cut each grapefruit half in half. Place on serving plates. Spoon the cream cheese mixture over each grapefruit portion.

Yield: 8 servings

Frosty Fruit Cup

6 ripe bananas, mashed
1 (20-ounce) can crushed
  pineapple
2 (17-ounce) cans apricots,
  chopped

2 tablespoons lemon juice
2 cups sugar
1 (16-ounce) can frozen orange
  juice concentrate, thawed
2 cups water

Combine the bananas, pineapple, apricots, lemon juice, sugar, orange juice concentrate and water in a large bowl and mix well.

Pour into 40 paper-lined muffin cups. Freeze until firm.

Yield: 40 servings

Cranberry Coffee Cake

1 (2-layer) yellow cake mix
1 (4-ounce) package vanilla
  instant pudding mix
5 eggs
½ cup bourbon

½ cup milk
½ cup vegetable oil
2 cups cranberries, chopped
1 cup chopped pecans
1 cup coconut

Combine the cake mix, pudding mix, eggs, bourbon, milk and oil in a large mixer bowl.

Beat at low speed until smooth. Beat at high speed for 3 minutes. Fold in the cranberries, pecans and coconut.

Pour the cranberry mixture into a greased and floured bundt pan.

Bake at 350 degrees for 55 minutes or until a wooden pick inserted in the cake comes out clean. Cool in the pan on a wire rack for 10 minutes. Invert onto a serving plate and cool completely. Garnish with confectioners' sugar.

Yield: 16 servings

Holiday Brunch Cake

2 cups flour
2 cups sugar
½ teaspoon salt
1 teaspoon baking powder
2 teaspoons baking soda
2 teaspoons cinnamon
1½ cups vegetable oil

1 teaspoon vanilla extract
4 eggs, room temperature
3 cups peeled, cored, shredded
  apples
½ cup raisins
½ cup chopped pecans
Pecan Frosting

Combine the flour, sugar, salt, baking powder, baking soda and cinnamon in a mixer bowl and mix well. Add the oil and vanilla and beat for 2 minutes or until smooth. Add the eggs. Beat for 2 minutes longer or until smooth. Stir in the apples, raisins and pecans.

Pour the batter into a greased bundt pan.

Bake in a preheated 350-degree oven for 50 minutes or until a wooden pick inserted in the cake comes out clean. Cool in the pan for 10 minutes.

Invert onto a serving plate. Drizzle the Pecan Frosting over the cooled cake. Decorate with maraschino cherries and chopped pecans.

Pecan Frosting

½ cup butter, softened
8 ounces cream cheese, softened
1 (16-ounce) package
  confectioners' sugar

1 teaspoon vanilla extract
Milk
1 cup chopped pecans

Cream the butter, cream cheese and confectioners' sugar in a mixer bowl until light and fluffy.

Add the vanilla and enough milk to make of spreading consistency. Stir in the pecans.

Yield: 16 servings

Philly Brunch Cake

½ cup butter or margarine
8 ounces cream cheese, softened
1¼ cups sugar
2 eggs
1 teaspoon vanilla extract
1¼ cups flour

1 teaspoon baking powder
1 teaspoon baking soda
¼ teaspoon salt
¼ cup milk
Brown Sugar Topping

Cream the butter, cream cheese and sugar in a mixer bowl until light and fluffy. Add the eggs 1 at a time, mixing well after each addition. Add the vanilla and mix well.

Combine the flour, baking powder, baking soda and salt in a bowl and mix well. Add to the creamed mixture alternately with the milk.

Pour into a greased and floured 9x13-inch cake pan. Sprinkle with Brown Sugar Topping.

Bake at 350 degrees for 35 to 40 minutes or until the cake tests done.

Brown Sugar Topping

⅓ cup packed brown sugar
⅓ cup flour

½ teaspoon cinnamon
2 tablespoons margarine

Combine the brown sugar, flour and cinnamon in a bowl and mix well.

Cut in the margarine until crumbly.

Yield: 15 servings

Overnight French Toast

¼ *cup butter*
1 *loaf of French bread*
6 *eggs*
1½ *cups milk*

¼ *cup sugar*
2 *tablespoons maple syrup*
1 *teaspoon vanilla extract*
½ *teaspoon salt*

Coat a 12x15-inch nonstick baking pan with the butter.

Cut the bread into ¾-inch-thick slices. Arrange in the prepared pan, fitting together tightly.

Combine the eggs, milk, sugar, maple syrup, vanilla and salt in a bowl and mix well. Pour over the bread. Turn each slice to coat both sides.

Refrigerate, covered, for 8 to 12 hours.

Bake at 400 degrees for 15 minutes. Turn over each slice. Bake for 15 minutes longer.

Yield: 8 servings

Brunch Pizza

1 (32-ounce) *package frozen hash*
   brown potatoes
9 *eggs*

½ *cup milk*
1½ *cups shredded Cheddar*
   cheese

Combine the potatoes and 2 of the eggs in a bowl and mix well. Spoon into a greased 9x13-inch baking pan. Bake in a preheated 400-degree oven for 20 minutes.

Combine the remaining 7 eggs and ½ cup milk in a microwave-safe bowl and mix well. Microwave on High for 6 minutes, stirring after 3 minutes. Spoon over the potato layer. Sprinkle the cheese over the egg layer. Bake for 10 minutes.

Yield: 15 servings

★ ★ ★ ★ ★

Embellishments

SUPPLEMENTAL & SUBSTANTIAL SALADS

*"When I moved into the White House, I went up to 185.
I've now hit an average of 175. I walk two miles most every
morning at a hundred and twenty-eight steps a minute.
I eat no bread but one piece of toast at breakfast, no butter,
no sugar, no sweets. Usually have fruit, one egg, a bacon
or sweet breads or ham or fish, and spinach, and another
nonfattening vegetable for lunch with fruit for dessert.
For dinner, I have a fruit cup, steak, a couple of nonfattening
vegetables and an ice, orange, pineapple or raspberry,
for dinner. So — I maintain my waistline and can wear
suits I bought in 1935."*

★ ★ ★ ★ ★

ruman held various positions before entering politics. He kept time for a Santa Fe railroad contractor, wrapped papers for the Kansas City Star, and was a clerk at the National Bank of Commerce. He spent ten years farming. "I did everything there was to do on a 600-acre farm," he says "from plowing, shucking corn, sowing and harvesting wheat to the care of all kinds of livestock." Harry served in World War I, eventually becoming captain of Battery D of the Missouri Field Artillery. He was well-liked and respected by his men as a brave and honorable leader.

In 1919, at the age of 35, Harry married Elizabeth "Bess" Virginia Wallace. Harry had met the golden-haired, blue-eyed girl who would become his wife in Sunday School at the age of 6. From a prominent Independence family, Bess Wallace was an athletic young woman who enjoyed baseball, dancing, ice-skating, tennis, and horseback riding. She and Harry went all through grade school and high school together. She took little notice of Harry until he returned a cake plate to her home, nine years after graduating from high school, when their courtship began in earnest. Although her mother disapproved of the match, feeling Harry would never amount to anything, the two were married at Trinity Episcopal Church in Independence. Harry later said, "…She was my sweetheart and ideal when I was a little boy — and she still is."

Truman, always a snappy dresser, opened a haberdashery across from the Muehlebach Hotel in Kansas City, with a soldier buddy, Eddie Jacobsen. In 1922, the business failed because of a depression. Ever proud, Truman refused to file bankruptcy and paid the last debt from the business as a senator fourteen years later.

Woodland Salad

1 pound asparagus, trimmed
1⅛ teaspoons salt
1 tablespoon fresh lemon juice
½ teaspoon Dijon mustard
3 tablespoons extra virgin olive oil
⅛ teaspoon coarsely ground pepper

4 ounces mushrooms, thinly sliced
½ cup loosely packed fresh Italian parsley leaves
1 ounce Parmesan cheese, freshly grated

Bring ½-inch-deep water to a boil in a large skillet. Add the asparagus and 1 teaspoon of the salt. Simmer, uncovered, for 7 to 10 minutes or until the asparagus is tender-crisp. Drain and cool in a single layer on paper towels.

Whisk the lemon juice and Dijon mustard in a large bowl. Whisk in the olive oil gradually. Stir in the pepper and remaining ⅛ teaspoon salt.

Add the asparagus to the olive oil mixture and toss to coat. Remove the asparagus, reserving the olive oil mixture. Arrange the asparagus on 4 salad plates.

Add the mushrooms and parsley to the reserved olive oil mixture. Toss to coat. Arrange the mushroom mixture over the asparagus. Sprinkle Parmesan cheese over the salad.

Yield: 4 servings

White Bean Salad

2 teaspoons minced garlic
1½ tablespoons coarse grain
   mustard
¼ cup lemon juice
1 teaspoon balsamic vinegar
½ cup chopped red onion

1 cup olive oil
1 (16-ounce) can white beans
4 ounces feta cheese, crumbled
½ cup pine nuts
¼ cup minced parsley

Combine the garlic, mustard, lemon juice, balsamic vinegar, onion and oil in a bowl and mix well.

Add the beans. Toss gently to coat.

Sprinkle the cheese, nuts and parsley over the salad.

Variations: May use dry beans soaked for several hours. May substitute red wine vinegar for the balsamic vinegar.

Yield: 6 servings

Broccoli Cashew Salad

1 head broccoli
1 pound bacon, cooked, crumbled
½ cup chopped red onion
1 cup mayonnaise

¼ cup milk
¼ cup (scant) sugar
1 cup cashews

Rinse the broccoli and pat dry. Cut into bite-size pieces. Combine the broccoli, bacon and onion in a bowl.

Combine the mayonnaise, milk and sugar in a separate bowl and mix well. Pour over the broccoli mixture and toss to coat. Sprinkle the cashews over the broccoli salad.

Variation: May substitute salad dressing for the mayonnaise and reduce the sugar to 3 tablespoons.

Yield: 8 servings

Off the Cob Salad

6 large ears white corn, husked
5 tablespoons olive oil
1 tablespoon minced garlic
½ cup packed thinly sliced fresh basil

5 plum tomatoes, seeded, chopped
3 tablespoons balsamic vinegar
Salt and pepper to taste

Cut the corn kernels from the cob into a bowl.

Heat 2 tablespoons of the oil in a large skillet over medium-high heat. Add the garlic. Sauté for 1 minute. Add the corn. Sauté for 5 minutes or until tender-crisp. Remove from heat.

Stir in half the basil. Pour the corn mixture into a large bowl.

Cool, stirring occasionally.

Add the tomatoes, vinegar, remaining 3 tablespoons of oil and remaining basil and mix well. Season with salt and pepper.

Chill, covered, for 3 to 8 hours.

Yield: 6 servings

Shoepeg Salad

1 (15-ounce) package frozen
   shoepeg corn, thawed, drained
1 cup finely chopped celery
1/4 cup finely chopped onion

1/4 cup finely chopped green or
   red bell pepper
1/4 cup mayonnaise
Salt and pepper to taste

Combine the corn, celery, onion, bell pepper, mayonnaise, salt and pepper in a bowl and mix well. Chill in the refrigerator.

Yield: 6 servings

Wild Craisin Corn Salad

1 (6-ounce) package long-grain
   and wild rice mix
2 cups fresh corn kernels
1 cup finely chopped celery
3/4 cup shredded carrots
3/4 cup craisins

2/3 cup sunflower seeds
1/2 cup finely chopped red onion
1/4 cup raspberry vinegar
1 tablespoon olive oil
1 tablespoon soy sauce

Prepare the rice mix using the package directions, omitting the butter. Let stand until completely cooled.

Combine the prepared rice, corn, celery, carrots, craisins, sunflower seeds, onion, vinegar, oil and soy sauce in a large bowl and mix well. Chill, covered, until ready to serve.

Yield: 8 servings

New New Potato Salad

1 pound new potatoes
½ cup sour cream
⅓ cup Dijon mustard
2 tablespoons white wine vinegar
1 tablespoon lemon juice

½ cup coarsely chopped fresh
　dill
Freshly ground black pepper
⅛ teaspoon white pepper

Cook the new potatoes in boiling salted water for 5 to 6 minutes or until tender but still firm; drain. Cool the potatoes. Cut into quarters.

Combine the sour cream, mustard, vinegar, lemon juice, dill, black pepper and white pepper in a bowl and mix well.

Add the potatoes and toss to coat.

Variation: May add sliced green onions.

Yield: 4 servings

Red and Bleu Potato Salad

3 pounds red potatoes
⅓ cup white wine
⅓ cup chicken broth
⅓ cup chopped parsley
⅓ cup sliced green onions

8 ounces bleu cheese, crumbled
¾ cup French dressing
⅓ cup crumbled crisp-fried
　bacon

Cook the red potatoes in boiling salted water for 5 to 6 minutes or until tender but still firm; drain. Cut into quarters.

Combine the wine, broth, parsley, and onions in a large bowl and mix well. Add the potatoes and toss to coat.

Combine the cheese and dressing in a bowl and mix well. Spoon over the potato mixture. Toss to coat.

Chill, covered, for 4 hours. Sprinkle the bacon over the salad. Serve immediately.

Yield: 10 servings

Herby Tomato Salad

3 medium tomatoes
1 cucumber
1 zucchini
1 green bell pepper
1 bunch green onions
1 bunch parsley

1 tablespoon minced mint leaves
½ clove of garlic, crushed
½ cup olive oil
Juice of 2 lemons
Salt and pepper to taste

Chop the tomatoes, cucumber and zucchini into ¼-inch pieces. Place in a large bowl.

Seed and chop the green pepper into ¼-inch pieces. Add to the tomato mixture.

Slice the green onions thinly. Add to the tomato mixture.

Chop the parsley. Add to the tomato mixture.

Add the mint, garlic, oil, lemon juice, salt and pepper and toss to mix.

Chill, covered, for 30 minutes.

Yield: 6 servings

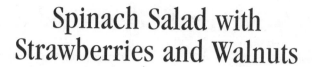

Spinach Salad with Strawberries and Walnuts

1 bunch of spinach
1 head Boston lettuce
1 head romaine lettuce
1 pint fresh strawberries

1 cup shredded Monterey Jack
 cheese
½ cup toasted English walnuts
Red Wine Vinegar Dressing

Wash the spinach and pat dry. Remove the stems. Wash and pat dry the Boston lettuce and romaine lettuce.

Tear the spinach, Boston and romaine lettuce into small pieces and place in a large bowl.

Wash and slice the strawberries. Add to the lettuce mixture. Add the cheese and walnuts.

Pour in the Red Wine Vinegar Dressing and toss to mix.

Red Wine Vinegar Dressing

½ cup red wine vinegar
1 cup vegetable oil
¾ cup sugar
2 cloves of garlic, minced

½ teaspoon salt
½ teaspoon paprika
¼ teaspoon white pepper

Combine the vinegar, oil, sugar, garlic, salt, paprika and pepper in a bowl and mix well.

Yield: 8 servings

Spinach Salad with Pears and Pecans

1 pound spinach
½ cup pecans
3 tablespoons olive oil
1 tablespoon balsamic vinegar

Salt and pepper to taste
3 green onions, sliced
2 pears, sliced

Wash the spinach and pat dry. Remove the stems.

Place the pecans on a baking sheet. Toast at 350 degrees for 5 minutes, stirring occasionally. Cool completely. Chop the pecans into small pieces.

Whisk the olive oil and vinegar in a small bowl. Add the salt and pepper. Combine the spinach and green onions in a large bowl. Pour the olive oil mixture over the spinach mixture and toss to coat. Sprinkle with the toasted pecans. Arrange the pears over the top.

Variation: May substitute tart apples for the pears.

Yield: 6 servings

Blue Ridge Salad

2 (10-ounce) packages frozen
  spinach, thawed
¼ to ½ cup chopped onion
½ cup chopped celery
1 cup shredded Cheddar cheese
4 hard-cooked eggs, chopped

¾ cup mayonnaise
½ teaspoon Tabasco sauce
½ teaspoon salt
1½ teaspoons lemon juice
2 teaspoons horseradish

Press the spinach to remove excess moisture. Combine the spinach, onion, celery, cheese and eggs in a bowl and mix well.

Combine the mayonnaise, Tabasco sauce, salt, lemon juice and horseradish in a bowl and mix well.

Pour the mayonnaise mixture over the spinach mixture and mix well. Shape into a ball and place in a serving bowl.

Yield: 6 servings

Crysler Coleslaw

**1 large head cabbage, finely
     shredded**
¾ cup mayonnaise
3 tablespoons sugar
**1½ tablespoons white wine
     vinegar**
⅓ cup vegetable oil
⅛ teaspoon garlic powder

⅛ teaspoon onion powder
⅛ teaspoon dry mustard
⅛ teaspoon celery salt
⅛ teaspoon pepper
1 tablespoon lemon juice
½ cup half-and-half
¼ teaspoon salt

Place the shredded cabbage in a bowl.

Combine the mayonnaise, sugar, vinegar and oil in a bowl and mix well.
Add the garlic powder, onion powder, dry mustard, celery salt, pepper,
lemon juice, half-and-half and salt and mix well.

Pour over the cabbage and mix well. Chill, covered, for 2 hours or longer.

Yield: 6 servings

Kraut Melange

2 (15-ounce) cans sauerkraut
½ cup chopped red bell pepper
½ cup chopped green bell pepper
1 cup chopped celery
4 carrots, thinly sliced

1 small onion, chopped
⅓ cup salad oil
1¼ cups sugar
½ cup cider vinegar

Combine the sauerkraut, bell peppers, celery, carrots and onion in a bowl
and mix well.

Combine the oil, sugar, vinegar and ⅓ cup water in a saucepan. Bring to a
boil. Remove from the heat and cool. Pour over the sauerkraut mixture and
mix well.

Chill, covered, for 8 to 12 hours or longer.

Yield: 6 servings

★　　　★　　　★　　　★　　　★

Artichoke Rice Salad

3 (6-ounce) jars marinated
   artichokes
4 cups chicken broth
2 cups uncooked long grain
   white rice
5 green onions, sliced

1 green bell pepper, seeded,
   chopped
1 red bell pepper, seeded, chopped
1 teaspoon curry
2 cups mayonnaise

Drain the artichokes, reserving the marinade.

Bring the broth to a boil in a saucepan. Stir in the rice. Bring to a boil and reduce the heat. Simmer, covered, for 20 minutes. Remove from heat.

Stir in the green onions, green pepper and red pepper.

Combine the reserved marinade, curry and mayonnaise in a bowl and mix well. Pour over the rice mixture and mix well.

Refrigerate, covered, until completely chilled.

Yield: 6 servings

Cashew Wild Rice Salad

1 (6-ounce) package of long-grain
and wild rice mix
1½ cups chopped cooked chicken
1½ cups seedless green grapes,
cut into halves

1 cup water chestnuts, sliced
½ to ¾ cup light mayonnaise
1 cup cashews

Cook the rice using the package directions. Cool completely.

Combine the rice, chicken, grapes, water chestnuts and mayonnaise in a bowl and mix well.

Chill, covered, for several hours. Stir in the cashews. Serve on a lettuce leaf with a fruit garnish and a roll.

Yield: 7 servings

"When a candidate for the presidency stands in front of the people,
the people get a chance to analyze his character in a way
they can't from television and radio."

★　　　★　　　★　　　★　　　★

Herbed Orzo Salad

1 pound orzo
3 cloves of garlic, sliced
3 tablespoons olive oil
5 teaspoons fresh chopped basil
¼ cup pine nuts, lightly toasted

2 tablespoons flat leaf parsley,
thinly sliced
¼ teaspoon salt
⅛ teaspoon pepper

Cook the orzo using the package directions.

Sauté the garlic in the oil in a small skillet over medium-high heat for 2 to 3 minutes. Discard the garlic.

Combine the orzo, garlic-flavored oil, basil, pine nuts, parsley, salt and pepper in a large bowl and toss gently to mix.

Chill, covered, for several hours. Bring to room temperature. Garnish with additional basil leaves.

Yield: 8 servings

Shrimp and Couscous Salad

½ cup couscous
1 pound peeled, deveined, cooked
shrimp, cut into halves
½ red bell pepper, chopped
½ yellow bell pepper, chopped
2 green onions, chopped

1 (14-ounce) can artichoke hearts
¼ cup mayonnaise
⅓ cup lemon juice
3 tablespoons chopped fresh dill
or chives
Salt and pepper to taste

Cook the couscous using the package directions. Let stand until completely cooled.

Combine the couscous, shrimp, bell peppers, green onions and artichoke hearts in a bowl and mix gently.

Combine the mayonnaise, lemon juice, dill, salt and pepper in a separate bowl and mix well. Pour over the shrimp mixture and mix well. Chill for 2 hours or longer.

Yield: 4 servings

Lemony Couscous Salad

1 (10-ounce) package couscous
1 small bunch spinach
3 tablespoons fresh lemon juice
¼ cup olive oil
⅛ teaspoon salt

Pepper to taste
1 leek, thinly sliced
3 tablespoons finely chopped
  fresh dill

Cook the couscous using the package directions.

Wash the spinach and pat dry. Remove the stems. Shred the spinach.

Combine the couscous, lemon juice, oil, salt and pepper in a bowl and mix well. Stir in the spinach, leek and dill.

Chill, covered, for 2 or more hours.

Variation: Add macadamia nuts or cashews.

Yield: 6 servings

Couscous Alfresco

1 (6-ounce) package couscous
½ cup sun-dried tomatoes, packed
  in oil, drained, chopped
2 cups packed chopped fresh
  spinach

1 tablespoon fresh lemon juice
¼ cup pine nuts, toasted
4 ounces feta cheese, crumbled

Cook the couscous using the package directions. Remove from heat. Stir in the sun-dried tomatoes. Let stand for 5 minutes.

Add the spinach a handful at a time to the couscous mixture, mixing well after each addition. Let stand, covered, for 2 minutes.

Stir the lemon juice into the couscous mixture. Sprinkle the pine nuts and feta cheese over the top. Garnish with parsley.

Yield: 4 servings

Southwest Confetti Salad

8 ounces orzo, cooked
1 (8-ounce) can sweet yellow
  corn, drained
1 (15-ounce) can black beans,
  rinsed, drained
1 red bell pepper, seeded, chopped
¼ cup cider vinegar

¼ cup balsamic vinegar
1 tablespoon Dijon mustard
1½ teaspoons cumin
1 teaspoon minced garlic
Salt and pepper to taste
1½ cups olive oil

Combine the orzo, corn, beans and red pepper in a bowl and mix well.

Combine the cider vinegar, balsamic vinegar, mustard, cumin, garlic, salt and pepper in a bowl and mix well. Whisk in the oil.

Pour over the pasta mixture and mix well.

Chill, covered, for several hours. Stir before serving.

Yield: 8 servings

Cropaico Salad

1 (6½-ounce) jar marinated
  artichoke hearts
1 cup chopped cooked chicken
1 (8-ounce) package chicken
  flavored Rice-a-Roni, prepared
1 (6-ounce) can black olives,
  drained

1 (10-ounce) package frozen peas,
  partially thawed
1 bunch green onions, sliced
1 cup Italian salad dressing
½ teaspoon curry powder

Drain the artichoke hearts, reserving the marinade. Chop the artichoke hearts.

Combine the chicken, rice, olives, peas, artichoke hearts and onions in a bowl and mix well.

Combine the salad dressing, reserved artichoke marinade and curry powder in a separate bowl and mix well. Pour over the chicken mixture and mix well.

Refrigerate, covered, until completely chilled.

Yield: 8 servings

Fruity Chicken Salad

1 (15¼-ounce) can pineapple
   tidbits
4 cups chopped cooked chicken
1 (11-ounce) can mandarin
   oranges, drained
1 (8-ounce) can sliced water
   chestnuts, drained
1 (2½-ounce) package sliced
   almonds, toasted

1 cup chopped celery
1 cup seedless green grapes,
   cut into halves
1½ cups mayonnaise
1 tablespoon soy sauce
1 teaspoon curry powder
1 (3-ounce) can chow mein
   noodles

Drain the pineapple, reserving 2 tablespoons of the juice.

Combine the pineapple, chicken, oranges, water chestnuts, almonds, celery
and grapes in a large bowl and mix well.

Combine the reserved pineapple juice, mayonnaise, soy sauce and curry
powder in a bowl and mix well. Pour over the chicken mixture and
mix well.

Refrigerate, covered, until chilled completely. Stir in the noodles. Serve
over lettuce leaves.

Yield: 8 servings

Wildly Delicious Turkey Salad

1 (6-ounce) package long-grain
   and wild rice mix
2⅓ cups water
1 cup firmly packed spinach
   leaves
2 cups chopped cooked turkey
4 ounces mushrooms, sliced
2 green onions, sliced

⅓ cup dry white wine
¼ cup vegetable oil
2 teaspoons sugar
¾ teaspoon salt
¼ teaspoon pepper
10 cherry tomatoes, cut into
   halves

Combine the rice, contents of seasoning packet and water in a saucepan. Bring to a boil. Simmer, covered, until all liquid is absorbed, about 25 minutes. Refrigerate, covered, until completely chilled.

Cut the spinach into thin strips.

Combine the rice, turkey, mushrooms, spinach and green onions in a bowl and mix well.

Whisk the wine, oil, sugar, salt and pepper in a small bowl. Pour over the rice mixture and mix well.

Chill, covered, until ready to serve. Arrange the tomatoes over the top.

Yield: 6 servings

Ham and Asparagus Tortellini Salad with Lemon Vinaigrette

*8 ounces asparagus, trimmed, cut
    into 1-inch pieces
1 (16-ounce) package frozen
    cheese tortellini
1 cup cubed cooked ham*

*¼ cup sliced green onions
Lemon Vinaigrette
2 cups strawberries, cut into
    halves*

Steam the asparagus in a steamer until tender-crisp; drain.

Cook the tortellini using the package directions.

Combine the cooked asparagus, cooked tortellini, ham and green onions in a bowl and mix gently.

Pour the Lemon Vinaigrette over the tortellini mixture. Toss gently to coat.

Chill, covered, for 30 minutes or longer. Stir in the strawberries.

Variation: Raspberries or blueberries may be substituted for the strawberries.

Lemon Vinaigrette

*3 tablespoons olive oil
3 tablespoons white wine vinegar
2 tablespoons frozen lemon
    concentrate, thawed*

*½ teaspoon grated lemon peel
¼ teaspoon salt
⅛ teaspoon pepper*

Combine the olive oil, vinegar, lemon concentrate, lemon peel, salt and pepper in a bowl and mix well.

Yield: 6 servings

Essentials

ENTICING SUSTENANCE

"It seems there's somebody for supper every night."

In 1922, Truman began his political career as an administrative judge of Jackson County. He was elected presiding judge in 1926 and reelected in 1930. Truman handled $60 million in public funds for new roads and bridges, yet the Truman farm was lost to the county on a mortgage. The local political establishment could not believe that a man with such responsibility could not save his mother's farm from a mortgage. It was only one of many testaments to the honesty that ran deep in the character of Harry Truman. His start in politics was largely due to a Kansas City political organization, but Judge Harry Truman was his own man.

On February 17, 1924, Mary Margaret Truman, the only child of Harry and Bess, arrived in the middle of a snowstorm. Harry was 40 and Bess was 39. For several months, four generations lived under one roof in Bess Truman's childhood home at 219 North Delaware, where the Trumans resided with Bess' mother and grandmother. The nurse who attended little Margaret's birth recalled Mr. Truman's devotion to his daughter as "remarkable and instantaneous." His devotion continued throughout his life. Margaret Truman Daniel later recalled, "At home he was the perfect father, full of jokes, and a constant tease. For a while he called me Skinny, because I was. He fretted endlessly over my health."

Beef and Bean Burritos

1 (2½-ounce) envelope taco
   seasoning mix
2 pounds London broil
1 cup chopped onion
1 tablespoon white vinegar
1 (4½-ounce) can chopped green
   chiles

1 (16-ounce) can refried beans
1½ cups shredded Monterey Jack
   cheese
12 (8-inch) flour tortillas

Rub the seasoning mix on both sides of the beef. Place the beef in a slow cooker sprayed with nonstick cooking spray. Add the onion, vinegar and chiles. Cook on Low for 9 hours.

Remove the beef, reserving the liquid mixture. Shred the beef by pulling apart with 2 forks. Return to the slow cooker.

Heat the beans to serving temperature in a saucepan.

Layer the beef mixture, beans and cheese in the center of each tortilla. Roll to enclose the filling. Serve each burrito with a dollop of sour cream.

Yield: 8 servings

Quick Cassoulet

1 pound lean ground beef
8 ounces cooked Polish sausage or
   kielbasa
½ cup chopped onion
1 clove of garlic, minced
1 (8-ounce) can tomato sauce

1 (15-ounce) can Great Northern
   beans, rinsed, drained
½ cup chopped celery
1 bay leaf
⅓ cup dry red wine
1 tablespoon flour

Place the beef in a 3-quart microwave-safe dish. Break up the beef. Remove the sausage casing. Cut the sausage into ½-inch slices. Layer over the beef. Sprinkle the onion and garlic over the sausage.

Microwave, covered, on High for 5 to 6 minutes or until the beef is browned and the onion is tender, stirring every 2 minutes; drain.

Stir in the tomato sauce, beans and celery. Add the bay leaf.

Whisk the wine and flour in a bowl. Add to the beef mixture and mix well.

Microwave on High for 6 to 8 minutes or until heated through, stirring after 3 minutes. Discard the bay leaf. Let stand for 5 minutes before serving.

Variation: Can be made on the stove in a large saucepan.

Yield: 10 servings

Mediterranean Veal Sauté

1 (2-pound) veal shoulder
2 tablespoons olive oil
2 medium onions, sliced
2 cloves of garlic, chopped
1 tablespoon flour
¾ cup red wine
1 teaspoon dried basil

1 pound tomatoes, peeled,
  chopped
Salt and pepper to taste
1 green bell pepper, seeded,
  chopped
1 (7-ounce) jar stuffed Spanish
  olives, sliced

Brown the veal in olive oil in a skillet. Add the onions and garlic. Sauté until the onions are tender. Stir in the flour. Turn the veal to coat.

Add the wine gradually, stirring constantly.

Add the basil, tomatoes, salt and pepper and mix well. Simmer until the veal is slightly pink in the center. Stir in the green pepper and olives.

Cook over low heat until the veal is tender and the green pepper is tender-crisp. Serve over rice.

Yield: 4 servings

Pork Loin and Kraut

4 pounds boneless pork loin
Garlic powder to taste
Salt to taste

Pepper to taste
Paprika to taste
2 pounds sauerkraut

Trim the fat from the pork. Place the pork in a roasting pan.

Sprinkle liberally with the garlic powder, salt, pepper and paprika.

Roast, covered, at 275 degrees for 1 hour.

Arrange the sauerkraut around the pork.

Roast, covered, for 15 minutes. Roast, uncovered, for 30 minutes or until the pork is cooked through.

Yield: 8 servings

Sesame Grilled Pork Tenderloin

1½ pounds pork tenderloin
¼ cup soy sauce
2 tablespoons sesame oil
3 tablespoons brown sugar
1 tablespoon dry sherry

4 cloves of garlic, minced
2 tablespoons sesame seeds,
   toasted
3 or 4 green onions, sliced

Place the pork tenderloin in a sealable plastic bag.

Combine the soy sauce, sesame oil, brown sugar, sherry, garlic, sesame seeds and onions in a bowl and mix well. Pour over the pork tenderloin and seal the bag. Marinate in the refrigerator for 8 hours or longer.

Drain the pork tenderloin. Grill over hot coals for 15 to 20 minutes or to 155 degrees on a meat thermometer, turning occasionally. Remove from the grill. Carve into medallions.

Yield: 6 servings

Mapled Pork Chops

6 pork chops
1 tablespoon dried minced onion
1 tablespoon vinegar
1 tablespoon Worcestershire sauce
1 teaspoon salt

½ teaspoon chili powder
⅛ teaspoon pepper
¼ cup maple syrup
¼ cup water

Place the pork chops in a single layer in a 9x13-inch baking dish. Combine the onion, vinegar, Worcestershire sauce, salt, chili powder, pepper, syrup and water in a bowl and mix well. Pour over the pork chops.

Bake the pork chops, covered, at 400 degrees for 45 minutes, basting occasionally with the syrup mixture. Bake, uncovered, for 15 minutes longer or until cooked through.

Yield: 6 servings

Pork Chops with Brandy Cream Sauce

6 (1-inch-thick) pork loin chops
Salt and pepper to taste
5½ tablespoons unsalted butter
2 tablespoons brown sugar
4 green apples, peeled, sliced

2 tablespoons brandy or apple
   brandy
¼ cup dry white wine
½ cup cream
⅛ teaspoon dried sage

Season the pork chops with salt and pepper. Brown in 2 tablespoons of the butter in a large skillet, turning once; drain well. Remove the pork chops to a warm plate.

Melt the remaining butter and 1 tablespoon of the brown sugar in the skillet. Add the apple slices. Sauté until golden. Stir in the brandy, wine, remaining brown sugar, cream and sage. Bring to a boil. Add the pork chops and any juices on the plate. Simmer, covered, for 20 minutes or until the pork chops are cooked through.

Remove the pork chops and apples to a serving platter. Cook the sauce until of the desired consistency. Pour over the pork chops and apples.

Yield: 6 servings

Honey-Chili Grilled Pork Chops with Peach Fritters

2 tablespoons chili powder
½ cup orange juice
Juice of 1 lemon
4 tablespoons honey
4 tablespoons ketchup
1 teaspoon ground cumin

4 tablespoons mango chutney
1½ pounds pork chops or
   boneless tenderloin
Salt and pepper
Peach Fritters

Combine the chili powder, orange juice, lemon juice, honey, ketchup, cumin and chutney in a large bowl. Add the pork chops, turning to coat.

Marinate, in the refrigerator, for 8 to 12 hours; drain.

Season the pork chops with salt and pepper. Preheat the grill to medium. Brush the grill rack with oil. Place the pork chops on the grill rack.

Grill over indirect heat until the pork chops have reached an internal temperature of 165 degrees, turning frequently. Serve with Peach Fritters.

Variation: May be broiled in an oven broiler or roasted in a 375-degree oven.

Yield: 4 servings

Peach Fritters

1 cup unbleached flour
1 teaspoon baking soda
¼ teaspoon salt
2 eggs
2 tablespoons honey
½ cup dark beer

½ cup milk
Vegetable oil for deep frying
6 ripe peaches, peeled,
cut into eighths
1 cup flour

Combine the unbleached flour, baking soda and salt in a bowl and mix well.

Combine the eggs, honey, beer and milk in a separate bowl and mix well. Whisk into the flour mixture until just moistened and lumpy. Let stand for 30 minutes.

Heat the oil to between 320 degrees and 340 degrees in a deep fryer or a cast-iron skillet.

Dredge the peaches in the flour in a shallow dish. Drop each peach into the batter. Place the coated peaches a few at a time into the hot oil.

Fry until golden brown and crisp. Drain on paper towels.

Yield: 4 servings

★　　　★　　　★　　　★　　　★

Rack of Lamb

⅓ cup fine dry bread crumbs
1 tablespoon olive oil
2 teaspoons fresh thyme leaves
1½ teaspoons ground cumin
1 small clove of garlic, minced

Salt and pepper to taste
1¼ pounds trimmed Frenched
  rack of lamb
1 teaspoon Dijon mustard

Combine the bread crumbs, oil, thyme, cumin and garlic in a bowl and mix well.

Sprinkle the salt and pepper over the lamb. Rub the mustard over the side of the lamb with fat. Pat the crumb mixture evenly over the mustard. Place the lamb crumb side up in a roasting pan.

Roast in a preheated 475-degree oven for 15 minutes or until a meat thermometer registers 130 to 135 degrees for medium rare. Let stand, uncovered, for 10 minutes. Cut the lamb between the ribs and serve.

Yield: 2 servings

Broiled Lamb Chops

8 lamb loin chops　　　　　　　**1 tablespoon crushed rosemary**
1 tablespoon olive oil　　　　　**½ teaspoon oregano**
1 clove of garlic, cut into halves　**Pepper to taste**

Rinse the lamb chops in hot water and pat dry.

Brush the lamb chops on both sides lightly with olive oil. Rub the garlic over the lamb chops. Sprinkle with the rosemary, oregano and pepper.

Place the lamb chops on a rack in a broiler pan. Broil in a preheated broiler for 10 to 12 minutes. Turn. Broil for 3 to 6 minutes longer for medium or until done to taste.

Yield: 4 servings

*"I would much rather be an honorable
public servant and known as such
than to be the richest man in the world."*

Blowin' Smoke Chicken Stix

1 (8-ounce) container plain
    yogurt
½ cup finely chopped onion
1 clove of garlic, minced
1½ teaspoons paprika
¾ teaspoon ground coriander

¾ teaspoon ground cumin
¼ teaspoon salt
8 boneless skinless chicken breast
    halves
2 large red bell peppers, seeded

Combine the yogurt, onion, garlic, paprika, coriander, cumin and salt in a bowl and mix well. Spread half the yogurt mixture in the bottom of an 8x12-inch baking dish.

Rinse the chicken and pat dry. Cut each chicken breast half cross grain into thirds.

Arrange the chicken in a single layer over the yogurt mixture. Spread the remaining yogurt mixture over the chicken.

Marinate, covered, in the refrigerator for 8 to 12 hours.

Cut the red peppers into 1¼-inch squares.

Thread the chicken and red peppers alternately onto 8 skewers.

Grill over hot coals for 12 to 18 minutes or until the chicken is cooked through, turning once.

Variation: May substitute 12 boneless skinless chicken thighs for the chicken breasts.

Yield: 8 servings

Chicken and Lemon Cream

4 chicken breasts
2 chicken bouillon cubes
1½ cups hot water
4 tablespoons butter
¾ cup flour
Salt and pepper to taste
1¼ teaspoons paprika

1 cup whipping cream
2 teaspoons lemon juice
1 teaspoon salt
½ cup milk
2 tablespoons olive oil
4 cups hot cooked rice

Rinse the chicken and pat dry. Cut the chicken into pieces.

Dissolve the bouillon cubes in the hot water in a bowl.

Melt the butter in a saucepan over medium heat. Whisk in ¼ cup of the flour, salt, pepper and ¼ teaspoon of the paprika. Whisk in the bouillon gradually.

Bring to a boil, stirring constantly. Stir in the cream.

Cook until heated through. Stir in the lemon juice. Remove from heat.

Combine the remaining ½ cup flour, salt and remaining 1 teaspoon of paprika in a shallow dish and mix well.

Dip the chicken in the milk in a bowl. Coat the chicken in the flour mixture.

Sauté in the olive oil in a skillet until golden brown on both sides and cooked through.

Divide the rice among 4 plates. Arrange the chicken over the rice. Top with the cream sauce.

Variation: May substitute 1½ cups chicken broth for the chicken bouillon cubes and hot water.

Yield: 4 servings

Chicken Breasts with Angel Hair

½ cup ranch-style salad dressing
1 tablespoon Dijon mustard
2 chicken breasts

¼ cup margarine or butter
¼ cup dry white wine
5 ounces angel hair pasta, cooked

Combine the salad dressing and mustard in a small bowl and mix well.

Rinse the chicken and pat dry.

Melt the margarine in a skillet over medium heat. Add the chicken. Sauté until golden brown and cooked through. Remove from skillet and keep warm.

Pour the wine into the skillet, stirring to deglaze the skillet. Cook for 5 minutes. Whisk in the salad dressing mixture. Cook until heated through.

Divide the pasta among 2 plates. Place the chicken over the pasta. Top with the sauce. Garnish with parsley.

Yield: 2 servings

Backyard Marinade

½ cup soy sauce
2½ tablespoons sesame oil
1½ tablespoons minced garlic
2 teaspoons lime juice

2 teaspoons rice wine vinegar
1½ teaspoons ground ginger
½ teaspoon sugar

Combine the soy sauce, sesame oil, garlic, lime juice, vinegar, ginger and sugar in a bowl and mix well.

Pour over chicken or pork. Marinate, covered, in the refrigerator for 30 minutes or longer.

Yield: 3 (¼-cup) servings

Chutney Chicken

4 boneless skinless chicken
  breasts
1 cup mayonnaise
1 cup sour cream

2 teaspoons curry powder
Juice of 2 lemons
¼ cup chutney
Pepper to taste

Place the chicken in a skillet. Cover with water. Bring the water to a boil. Simmer until the chicken is cooked through; drain. Place in a baking dish.

Combine the mayonnaise and sour cream in a bowl and mix well. Stir in the curry powder and lemon juice.

Cover the chicken with the mayonnaise mixture. Spoon the chutney over the mayonnaise mixture. Sprinkle with pepper. Bake at 450 degrees for 15 minutes. Serve over rice or couscous.

Yield: 8 servings

Clubhouse Chicken

1 (4-pound) whole chicken or
  6 chicken breasts
1 teaspoon salt
2 cups milk
2 (8-ounce) packages cream
  cheese

1 teaspoon garlic salt
¼ teaspoon garlic powder
1½ cups grated Parmesan cheese
2 (10-ounce) packages frozen
  chopped broccoli, partially
  cooked

Cook the chicken in salted water to cover in a large stockpot until tender; drain. Chop the chicken, discarding skin and bones.

Combine the milk, cream cheese and seasonings in a double boiler. Cook over boiling water until smooth. Stir in ¾ cup of the Parmesan cheese.

Layer the broccoli, 1 cup of the sauce, chicken and remaining sauce in a greased 9x13-inch baking dish. Sprinkle with remaining Parmesan cheese. Bake at 350 degrees for 30 minutes. Let stand for 5 minutes or until firm.

Yield: 15 servings

Chicken Spiedini

**4 to 5 pounds boneless skinless
 chicken breasts
1 to 1½ cups extra virgin olive
 oil
1 tablespoon crushed red pepper
2 cloves of garlic, crushed**

**3 cups bread crumbs
2 cups grated Parmesan cheese
½ cup chopped parsley
Pepper to taste
3 or 4 cloves of garlic, minced
Amogio**

Rinse the chicken and pat dry. Pound to ½-inch thickness between sheets of waxed paper. Cut into 1-inch-wide strips 4 to 5 inches long.

Combine the olive oil, crushed red pepper and crushed garlic in a large bowl and mix well. Add the chicken, stirring to coat completely.

Marinate, covered, in the refrigerator for 1 hour or longer.

Combine the bread crumbs, cheese, parsley, pepper and minced garlic in a bowl and mix well to form "modiga." Remove the chicken from the marinade. Dredge in the modiga to coat both sides.

Roll up each coated strip; thread onto skewers, 6 to 8 per skewer. Roll the threaded skewers in the modiga, pressing onto the chicken. Place the skewers on a rack in a broiler pan.

Broil until the chicken is cooked through and dark golden brown, turning frequently. Remove the chicken from the skewers. Top with a generous amount of Amogio. Garnish with lemon wedges.

Amogio

**1½ cups olive oil
6 tablespoons melted margarine
¼ to ½ teaspoon salt**

**2 to 4 cloves of garlic
Juice of 2 large lemons**

Combine the olive oil, margarine, salt, garlic and lemon juice in a blender container. Process until well blended.

Yield: 16 servings

Comfort Chicken

2 cups sliced peeled carrots
1 red bell pepper, seeded,
   cut into strips
3 tablespoons butter
¼ cup flour
2 cups chicken broth
1 cup milk
1 tablespoon lemon juice

3 chicken breasts, cooked,
   chopped
1 (10-ounce) package frozen peas
   with pearl onions
2 cups biscuit mix
⅔ cup milk
¾ cup shredded Cheddar cheese

Steam the carrots and red pepper in a steamer for 5 to 8 minutes or until tender-crisp; drain.

Melt the butter in a skillet over low heat. Add the flour. Cook for 1 minute, stirring constantly. Whisk in the chicken broth and milk gradually. Cook over medium heat until of the desired consistency and bubbly. Remove from heat.

Stir in the lemon juice. Add the chicken, carrot mixture and peas and mix well. Spoon into a lightly greased 7x11-inch baking pan.

Combine the biscuit mix and milk in a small bowl and mix well. Knead the dough on a floured surface. Roll into a rectangle. Sprinkle with the cheese. Roll as for a jelly roll, sealing the edge and ends.

Cut the roll into 1-inch slices. Arrange over the chicken mixture.

Bake at 400 degrees for 30 minutes or until the top is golden brown.

Yield: 4 servings

Honey Basil Chicken

½ cup raspberry vinegar
1½ tablespoons Dijon mustard
2 tablespoons soy sauce
2 tablespoons honey
2 tablespoons minced fresh basil

1 teaspoon dried thyme
Freshly ground pepper
4 boneless skinless chicken breast
  halves

Combine the vinegar, mustard, soy sauce, honey, basil, thyme and pepper in a shallow dish and mix well.

Rinse the chicken and pat dry. Add to the vinegar mixture.

Marinate in the refrigerator for 30 minutes to 2 hours.

Preheat the grill to medium. Drain the chicken, reserving the marinade. Grill the chicken for 8 minutes or until cooked through, turning once. Remove to a platter and keep warm.

Pour the reserved marinade in a saucepan. Bring to a boil. Cook until the marinade is reduced by half. Pour over the chicken.

Variation: Place the chicken in a baking dish. Pour the marinade over the chicken. Bake in the oven at 350 degrees for 30 minutes.

Yield: 4 servings

Hot Chicken

1 (10-ounce) can cream of mushroom soup	3 tablespoons lemon juice
1 (10-ounce) can cream of chicken soup	2 cups chopped cooked chicken
1 (10-ounce) can cream of celery soup	1½ cups chopped yellow onion
	2 cups chopped celery
2 cups mayonnaise	2 (8-ounce) cans water chestnuts
	½ cup slivered almonds
	4½ ounces chow mein noodles

Combine the mushroom soup, chicken soup, celery soup, mayonnaise and lemon juice in a bowl and mix well.

Stir in the chicken, onion, celery, water chestnuts, almonds and chow mein noodles. Spoon into a 9x13-inch baking dish.

Bake at 350 degrees for 30 to 40 minutes. Garnish with additional chow mein noodles.

Yield: 10 servings

Garlic Marinade

1½ cups canola oil	10 drops of Tabasco sauce
½ cup lemon juice	6 cloves of garlic, crushed
1 teaspoon coarsely ground pepper	1 cup grated Parmesan cheese
	1 teaspoon salt

Combine the oil, lemon juice, pepper, Tabasco sauce, garlic, cheese and salt in a jar and mix well. Chill, covered, for 8 hours or longer. Shake and pour over chicken. Marinate, covered, in the refrigerator for 30 minutes or longer.

Yield: 10 (¼-cup) servings

Knoepker's Creamed Chicken

1 (10-ounce) package puff pastry
   shells
2 (3-ounce) cans sliced
   mushrooms
1 cup chopped green bell pepper
1 cup butter
1 cup flour

2 teaspoons salt
½ teaspoon pepper
2 cups cream or evaporated milk
2½ cups chicken broth
4 cups chopped cooked chicken
2 (4-ounce) jars chopped
   pimentos, drained

Prepare the pastry shells using the package directions.

Drain the mushrooms, reserving ½ cup of the liquid.

Sauté the mushrooms and green pepper in the butter in a skillet. Stir in the flour. Cook until bubbly, stirring constantly.

Add the salt, pepper, cream, broth, chicken, pimentos and reserved mushroom liquid and mix well.

Serve over the prepared puff pastry shells.

Yield: 6 servings

Piggyback Chicken Fingers

**2 pounds boneless skinless
chicken breasts
1½ cups buttermilk**

**1 teaspoon vegetable or olive oil
1 cup bread crumbs
Salt and pepper to taste**

Rinse the chicken and pat dry. Place in a medium bowl. Pour the buttermilk over the chicken.

Marinate, covered, in the refrigerator for 30 minutes or up to 24 hours.

Coat a baking pan with the oil. Combine the bread crumbs, salt and pepper in a shallow dish and mix well.

Drain the chicken. Cut into thin, finger-size strips. Dredge in the bread crumbs, shaking off the excess. Arrange in the baking pan.

Bake in a preheated 400-degree oven for 15 minutes or until golden brown and cooked through, turning after 10 minutes. May be served warm or chilled. Serve with lemon wedges.

Yield: 6 servings

Summer Lime Chicken Breast and Stir-Fry Broccoli with Sesame and Walnuts

4 boneless skinless chicken breasts
⅓ cup olive oil
Juice of 3 limes
4 cloves of garlic, minced
3 tablespoons chopped fresh cilantro

½ teaspoon salt
½ teaspoon freshly ground black pepper
6 bell peppers, yellow, red or orange
Stir-Fry Broccoli with Sesame and Walnuts (page 85)

Rinse the chicken and pat dry. Pound to ½-inch thickness between sheets of waxed paper.

Combine the oil, lime juice, garlic, cilantro, salt and pepper in a large bowl. Add the chicken and stir to coat. Marinate, covered, in the refrigerator for 2 hours or longer. Drain the chicken. Place on a grill over hot coals. Cook for 10 minutes or until cooked through, turning once.

Seed and cut the peppers into wedges. Brush lightly with olive oil. Sprinkle with salt and pepper. Grill until tender-crisp. Serve with Stir-Fry Broccoli with Sesame and Walnuts.

Yield: 4 servings

Stir-Fry Broccoli with Sesame and Walnuts

1½ teaspoons sesame oil
½ teaspoon chili oil
Garlic powder to taste
¼ cup chopped walnuts

4 cups fresh broccoli, coarsely
chopped
1 tablespoon low-sodium soy
sauce

Combine the sesame oil, chili oil and garlic powder in a wok and mix well. Cook over high heat until hot. Reduce the heat to medium.

Add the walnuts and broccoli. Cook for 4 minutes, stirring occasionally. Stir in the soy sauce. Cook, covered, for 1 minute.

Yield: 4 servings

R & B Chicken

2 to 3 boneless skinless chicken
breasts
1¼ cups water
4 teaspoons instant chicken
bouillon

1 cup rice
1 (14-ounce) can Mexican-style
stewed tomatoes
1 or 2 (15-ounce) cans black
beans, drained, rinsed

Rinse the chicken and pat dry. Cut into small pieces.

Sauté in a skillet coated with nonstick cooking spray until just pink in the center.

Stir in the water, chicken bouillon, rice, tomatoes and black beans.

Simmer, covered, for 20 minutes, stirring occasionally. Serve with warm flour tortillas.

Yield: 4 servings

Pasta Dijon Au Artichokes

1 pound chicken breasts
4 ounces Brie
2 tablespoons olive oil
2 cloves of garlic, minced
1 (10-ounce) package frozen
artichokes

⅔ cup half-and-half
¼ cup Dijon mustard
1 teaspoon Italian herbs
5 green onions, chopped
1 pound pasta, cooked, drained

Rinse the chicken and pat dry. Cut into pieces.

Remove the rind from the Brie. Cut into pieces.

Sauté the chicken and garlic in the olive oil in a skillet. Stir in the artichokes. Cook until tender-crisp.

Add the Brie, half-and-half, mustard and herbs. Cook until the Brie melts, stirring constantly. Stir in the green onions and hot pasta.

Yield: 4 servings

Lime and Sesame Roasted Cornish Hens

2 (1½-pound) Cornish hens,
    split
⅓ cup soy sauce
¼ cup vegetable oil
3 cloves of garlic, sliced

2 tablespoons sesame seeds,
    lightly toasted
1 tablespoon brown sugar
2 teaspoons ground ginger
3 tablespoons lime juice

Place the hens breast side down in a large shallow dish.

Combine the soy sauce, oil, garlic, sesame seeds, brown sugar, ginger and lime juice in a blender container. Process until well blended, stopping once to scrape down the sides. Pour over the hens.

Marinate, covered, in the refrigerator for 8 hours, turning occasionally. Remove the hens, reserving the marinade.

Pour the marinade into a small saucepan. Bring to a boil. Cook for 2 to 3 minutes. Remove from heat.

Place the hens breast side up in a lightly greased 9x13-inch baking pan.

Bake at 400 degrees for 45 minutes or until cooked through, basting occasionally with the cooked marinade. Garnish with additional toasted sesame seeds and lime wedges.

Yield: 4 servings

Midway Stew

1 red bell pepper
1 green bell pepper
⅓ cup ketchup
⅓ cup packed brown sugar
3 (14-ounce) cans stewed
   tomatoes

2 (16-ounce) cans butter beans
2 (16-ounce) cans kidney beans
1 onion, sliced
1 to 2 pounds turkey kielbasa,
   sliced

Seed the red pepper and green pepper and cut into strips.

Combine the ketchup, brown sugar and tomatoes in a bowl and mix well. Spoon into a slow cooker.

Stir in the butter beans, kidney beans, onion, red pepper, green pepper and kielbasa.

Cook on Low for 4 to 6 hours. Increase heat to High. Cook for 2 to 3 hours longer.

Yield: 6 servings

*"Three things can ruin a man: power, money, and women.
I never wanted power, I never had any money, and the only
woman in my life is up at the house right now."*

Roasted Salmon and Vegetables

¼ cup olive oil
4 carrots, julienned
3 leeks (white and pale green parts), thinly sliced
1 small fennel bulb, finely chopped
1 cup clam juice
½ cup dry white wine
2 bay leaves

2 tablespoons chopped fresh parsley
2 tablespoons chopped fresh tarragon
2 tablespoons chopped fresh chives
10 (5- to 6-ounce) skinless salmon fillets
Salt and pepper to taste

Heat the oil in a large heavy saucepan over medium-high heat. Add the carrots, leeks and fennel. Sauté for 7 minutes or until tender-crisp. Add the clam juice, wine and bay leaves and mix well.

Bring to a boil. Stir in the parsley, tarragon and chives. Spoon into a large baking pan.

Arrange the salmon over the vegetable mixture. Sprinkle with salt and pepper.

Bake in a preheated 400-degree oven for 12 to 15 minutes or until the fish flakes easily. Discard the bay leaves.

Yield: 10 servings

Succulent Salmon

6 (8-ounce) boneless skinless
   salmon fillets
2 tablespoons butter
2 tablespoons flour
1 cup milk
4 ounces shredded Cheddar cheese
8 tablespoons grated Parmesan
   cheese

Dash of red pepper sauce
1/2 teaspoon Worcestershire sauce
3/4 cup sour cream
3/4 cup mayonnaise
Seasoned salt to taste
Paprika
2 ounces slivered almonds,
   toasted

Rinse the fish and drain. Set aside.

Melt the butter in a skillet. Stir in the flour. Cook over medium heat until the mixture turns golden brown, stirring constantly. Whisk in the milk. Cook until of the desired consistency, stirring constantly.

Stir in the Cheddar cheese and 2 tablespoons of the Parmesan cheese. Cook until the cheeses melt, stirring constantly.

Stir in the red pepper sauce and Worcestershire sauce. Cook until heated through; do not boil. Set aside and keep warm.

Combine the sour cream and mayonnaise in a small bowl and mix well. Pour 1/4 inch of water into a 9x13-inch baking pan. Sprinkle the fish with seasoned salt and place in the baking pan.

Spoon equal amounts of the sour cream mixture over the fish. Sprinkle each fillet with 1 tablespoon of the remaining Parmesan cheese. Sprinkle with paprika.

Bake in a preheated 450-degree oven for 15 minutes or until the fish flakes easily.

Spoon equal amounts of the Cheddar cheese sauce on 6 plates. Swirl each plate to coat the surface with sauce. Place a fillet over the sauce. Top with the almonds.

Yield: 6 servings

Clam Tetrazzini

2 (8-ounce) cans minced clams
1½ to 2 cups light cream or
    evaporated milk
¼ cup margarine
¼ cup flour
⅛ teaspoon salt
¼ teaspoon thyme
¼ teaspoon nutmeg
2 to 3 drops of Tabasco sauce

2 tablespoons sherry
1 egg yolk, beaten
1 (7-ounce) jar mushrooms
1 pound linguine, cooked
½ cup grated Parmesan cheese
¼ cup bread crumbs
2 tablespoons dried chopped
    parsley

Drain the clams, reserving the juice. Add enough cream to the reserved clam juice to equal 2 cups.

Melt the margarine in a saucepan. Add the flour, stirring until smooth. Whisk in the cream mixture gradually. Bring to a boil, stirring constantly. Boil for 1 minute. Remove from heat. Stir in the salt, thyme, nutmeg, Tabasco and sherry.

Stir a small amount of the hot mixture into the beaten egg yolk. Stir the egg yolk into the hot mixture. Add the mushrooms and clams and mix well.

Layer the pasta and clam sauce ½ at a time in a 9x13-inch baking pan. Sprinkle with the Parmesan cheese, bread crumbs and parsley.

Bake in a preheated 400-degree oven for 20 minutes or until heated through.

Yield: 6 servings

Saul's Flaming Swordfish

¼ cup tequila
1 tablespoon Triple Sec
¼ cup olive oil
½ cup lime juice

3 cloves of garlic, minced
1 tablespoon pepper
4 swordfish steaks

Place the swordfish in a shallow dish.

Combine the tequila, Triple Sec, oil, lime juice, garlic and pepper in a bowl and mix well. Pour over the swordfish.

Marinate, covered, in the refrigerator for 2 to 4 hours. Drain the swordfish.

Grill over hot coals for 10 to 12 minutes or until the fish flakes easily, turning once.

Yield: 4 servings

Scallops au Gratin

2 cups sliced zucchini
¾ cup julienned carrots
2 tablespoons butter
¼ cup flour
⅔ cup heavy cream
1 pound scallops, rinsed, drained

5 tablespoons grated Parmesan cheese
¼ teaspoon salt
¼ teaspoon pepper
2 tablespoons dry white wine

Sauté the zucchini and carrots in the butter in a skillet until tender-crisp. Sprinkle with the flour. Toss to coat. Pour in the cream. Cook over medium heat for 1 minute, stirring constantly.

Add the scallops, 2 tablespoons of the cheese, salt and pepper. Bring to a boil. Remove from the heat. Stir in the wine. Spoon into a 9-inch quiche dish. Sprinkle with the remaining cheese. Bake at 375 degrees for 20 to 30 minutes.

Yield: 6 servings

Sausalito Scallops

2 cloves of garlic, minced
3 tablespoons olive oil
1 pound large bay scallops
2 medium tomatoes, cut into
   1-inch pieces
8 ounces mushrooms, sliced
1 teaspoon basil

1 teaspoon thyme
¼ cup dry vermouth
Salt and pepper to taste
1 (9-ounce) package fresh angel
   hair pasta, cooked
½ cup grated Parmesan cheese

Sauté the garlic in the olive oil in a skillet for 2 minutes.

Add the scallops. Sear until lightly browned. Reduce the heat to medium. Remove the scallops.

Add the tomatoes, mushrooms, basil and thyme to the skillet. Cook until the tomatoes are crushed and the mushrooms are tender. Stir in the vermouth and scallops.

Cook for 2 minutes. Season with salt and pepper.

Divide the pasta among 4 plates. Spoon the scallop mixture over the pasta. Sprinkle with the Parmesan cheese.

Yield: 4 servings

Scallops, Zucchini and Tomatoes over Penne

8 ounces sea scallops
1½ teaspoons plus 1 tablespoon
  olive oil
1 clove of garlic, crushed
2 (½-inch-thick) slices French
  bread
1 clove of garlic, minced
1 small red onion, chopped

1 small zucchini, chopped
1 cup crushed fresh or canned
  tomatoes
2 tablespoons minced fresh basil
1 tablespoon lemon juice
Salt and pepper to taste
6 ounces hot cooked penne

Drain the scallops, reserving the juice.

Heat 1½ teaspoons of the olive oil in a skillet. Add the crushed garlic. Sauté for 1 minute. Add the bread slices. Sauté for 1 to 2 minutes per side or until golden. Remove the bread. Discard the garlic.

Add the remaining 1 tablespoon olive oil to the skillet. Add the minced garlic, onion and zucchini. Sauté for 5 minutes or until the vegetables are golden.

Add the scallops. Sauté for 1 to 2 minutes.

Stir in the reserved scallop juice, tomatoes and basil. Simmer for 5 minutes.

Stir in the lemon juice. Season lightly with salt and generously with pepper.

Divide the pasta among 2 plates. Spoon the scallop mixture over the pasta. Cut the bread into ½-inch cubes. Sprinkle over the top.

Yield: 2 servings

Pasta with Shrimp and Feta

2 teaspoons olive oil
½ onion, chopped
1 clove of garlic, minced
1 (14½-ounce) can diced
*   tomatoes*
4 ounces cooked shrimp
3½ cups pasta, such as rotelli or
*   rotini*

2 tablespoons finely chopped
*   basil*
2 tablespoons lemon juice
½ cup crumbled feta cheese
⅛ teaspoon cayenne
Freshly ground black pepper
*   to taste*

Heat the olive oil in a large skillet over medium heat. Add the onion and garlic. Sauté for 5 minutes or until tender.

Add the tomatoes. Simmer for 10 minutes or until of the desired consistency.

Stir in the shrimp. Cook until heated through.

Cook the pasta using the package directions; drain. Add the pasta to the shrimp sauce.

Add the basil, lemon juice, feta, cayenne and black pepper and mix well.

Yield: 2 servings

Shrimp Pizza

1 (1-crust) package pizza
   crust mix
½ cup ricotta cheese
1 to 2 teaspoons horseradish
   sauce
¼ cup chopped green onions

5 or 6 slices bacon, crisp-fried,
   crumbled
1 (12-ounce) package frozen
   cooked shrimp, thawed
8 ounces mozzarella cheese,
   shredded

Prepare the pizza dough using the package directions.

Combine the ricotta cheese and horseradish sauce in a bowl and mix well. Spread over the pizza dough. Sprinkle with the green onions and bacon. Arrange the shrimp over the onions and bacon. Sprinkle with the mozzarella cheese. Bake in a preheated 425-degree oven for 15 minutes.

Yield: 2 servings

Shrimp Creole

2 tablespoons flour
2 slices bacon, chopped
⅔ cup chopped green onions
1 (10-ounce) bottle of clam juice
1 (16-ounce) can crushed tomatoes
1 bay leaf
1 teaspoon Worcestershire sauce

¼ teaspoon thyme
Salt and pepper to taste
1 teaspoon grated lemon rind
1 pound uncooked deveined
   shrimp
1 (10-ounce) package frozen okra
2 cups hot cooked white rice

Brown the flour in a small skillet over low heat. Fry the bacon in a Dutch oven until partially cooked. Stir in the onions. Sprinkle the browned flour over the onions and mix well. Add the clam juice, whisking constantly. Cook over low heat until smooth and thick, whisking constantly.

Stir in the tomatoes, bay leaf, Worcestershire sauce, thyme, salt, pepper, lemon rind and shrimp. Cook for 10 minutes. Add the okra. Stir, breaking the okra into pieces. Bring to a boil. Reduce heat. Simmer for 15 minutes. Divide the rice among 4 plates. Remove the bay leaf from the shrimp mixture. Spoon the shrimp mixture over the rice.

Yield: 4 servings

Smith's Shrimp Sauté

1 cup orzo
1 tablespoon plus 1 teaspoon
  olive oil
Salt and freshly ground pepper
  to taste
2 cloves of garlic, minced
20 large shrimp, peeled

¼ cup finely chopped Italian
  parsley
Juice and grated rind of 1 lemon
1 cup dry white wine
5 tablespoons unsalted butter
1 tablespoon capers, rinsed

Cook the orzo using the package directions; drain. Toss with 1 teaspoon of the oil, salt and pepper. Cover to keep warm.

Heat 1 tablespoon oil in a large skillet. Add the garlic. Cook over low heat for 1 minute.

Add the shrimp, salt, pepper and 2 tablespoons of the parsley. Cook for 6 to 7 minutes or until the shrimp become pink, turning once. Remove from the pan and keep warm.

Add the lemon juice and wine to the skillet. Bring to a boil. Simmer until reduced by half. Remove from heat.

Stir in the remaining 2 tablespoons of parsley, butter, grated lemon rind and capers.

Divide the orzo among 4 plates. Place the shrimp over the orzo. Spoon the sauce over the shrimp.

Yield: 4 servings

Amer's Red Hot Pasta

1¼ cups olive oil
2 cups chopped red onions
½ cup chopped celery
½ cup chopped carrots
3 cloves of garlic
½ teaspoon salt

⅛ teaspoon pepper
1 (14½-ounce) can diced
  tomatoes
1 teaspoon red pepper flakes
1½ pounds penne pasta
10 leaves fresh basil

Heat the oil in a medium saucepan. Add the onion, celery, carrots, garlic, salt and pepper. Cook over medium-high heat for 15 to 17 minutes or until tender-crisp, stirring constantly.

Stir in the tomatoes and red pepper flakes. Reduce the heat to medium-low. Cook for 30 minutes.

Cook the pasta using the package directions; drain.

Add the basil leaves to the tomato mixture. Pour into a blender container and process until well blended.

Combine the sauce and pasta in a bowl and toss to coat.

Yield: 6 servings

Lemon Pasta

1 pound angel hair pasta
2 cloves of garlic, minced
¼ cup olive oil
1 (16-ounce) can tomatoes,
  chopped or sliced

⅓ cup fresh lemon juice
1 teaspoon oregano
1 teaspoon basil
4 ounces feta cheese, crumbled

Cook the pasta using the package directions; drain. Cover to keep warm.

Sauté the garlic in the olive oil in a skillet for 2 to 3 minutes. Add the tomatoes. Simmer for 1 minute. Stir in the lemon juice. Simmer for 2 minutes. Stir in the oregano and basil.

Place the pasta in a bowl. Spoon the sauce over the pasta. Sprinkle with the cheese.

Yield: 4 servings

Egg Noodles in Poppy Seed Sauce

8 ounces medium egg noodles
2 tablespoons olive oil
8 ounces mushrooms, sliced
1 onion, chopped
¼ teaspoon salt

½ cup dry white wine
¼ cup sour cream
½ cup plain nonfat yogurt
1 tablespoon poppy seeds
¼ teaspoon cayenne pepper

Cook the egg noodles in boiling salted water in a saucepan using package directions; drain. Cover to keep warm.

Heat 1 tablespoon of the oil in a skillet. Add the mushrooms and onion. Sprinkle with the salt. Cook until the mushrooms and onion are browned, stirring frequently. Pour in the wine. Cook until the liquid is almost absorbed, stirring frequently. Remove from heat. Mix the sour cream, yogurt, poppy seeds, remaining oil and cayenne pepper in a bowl.

Combine the cooked noodles, mushroom mixture and poppy seed mixture in a large serving bowl and toss to mix.

Yield: 2 servings

Legislative Lasagna

1 (10-ounce) package frozen
  spinach
8 ounces lasagna noodles
½ cup chopped onion
2 cloves of garlic
2 tablespoons butter
2 eggs, beaten
1 (24-ounce) carton cottage
  cheese or ricotta cheese

½ cup grated Parmesan cheese
2 tablespoons chopped fresh
  parsley
10 ounces Monterey Jack cheese,
  shredded
2 cups shredded Cheddar cheese

Cook the spinach using the package directions; drain.

Cook the pasta using the package directions; drain.

Sauté the onion and garlic in butter in a skillet until the onion is translucent.

Combine the eggs, cottage cheese, Parmesan cheese, parsley and Monterey Jack cheese in a bowl and mix well. Add the onion mixture and spinach and mix well.

Alternate layers of the spinach mixture, pasta and Cheddar cheese in a greased 9x13-inch baking dish until all the ingredients are used.

Bake at 350 degrees for 30 to 45 minutes.

Yield: 10 servings

Linguine with Two Sauces

2 teaspoons olive oil
2 cloves of garlic, minced
1 tablespoon chopped fresh basil
¾ teaspoon pepper
½ teaspoon salt
2 (14½-ounce) cans diced Italian
  tomatoes
4 cups sliced cremini or button
  mushrooms

½ cup flour
2 cups low-fat milk
1 cup shredded low-fat Swiss
  cheese
½ cup dry white wine
8 cups hot cooked linguine
¼ cup grated Parmesan cheese

Heat the oil over medium heat in a large nonstick skillet. Sauté the garlic for 30 seconds. Stir in the basil, ¼ teaspoon of the pepper, ¼ teaspoon of the salt and the tomatoes.

Cook over low heat for 20 minutes, stirring occasionally. Set aside.

Heat a large saucepan coated with nonstick cooking spray over medium-high heat. Add the mushrooms. Cook for 5 minutes. Remove the mushrooms to a bowl.

Add the flour to the saucepan. Whisk in the milk gradually. Cook over medium heat for 3 minutes or until of the desired consistency, stirring constantly. Stir in the Swiss cheese, wine, remaining ½ teaspoon pepper and remaining ¼ teaspoon salt.

Cook until the cheese melts, stirring constantly. Remove from heat. Stir in the cooked mushrooms.

Combine the pasta and mushroom sauce in a bowl and toss to coat.

Spoon into a 9x13-inch baking dish coated with nonstick cooking spray. Spread the tomato sauce over the pasta mixture. Sprinkle with the Parmesan cheese.

Bake in a preheated 350-degree oven, covered, for 20 minutes. Bake, uncovered, for 5 minutes longer.

Yield: 8 servings

Pasta with Tomatoes, Mozzarella and Basil

8 ounces mozzarella cheese
1½ pounds plum tomatoes,
  seeded, coarsely chopped
3 tablespoons extra-virgin olive
  oil

2 teaspoons red wine vinegar
Salt and pepper to taste
½ cup chopped fresh basil
12 ounces penne pasta

Cut the mozzarella into ½x1-inch strips.

Combine the mozzarella, tomatoes, oil, vinegar, salt and pepper in a bowl and mix well. Let stand for 1 hour at room temperature. Stir in the basil.

Cook the pasta using the package directions; drain.

Combine the pasta and the tomato mixture in a bowl and toss gently to coat. Season with salt and pepper.

Yield: 4 servings

Pasta Baked with Stilton and Port

2 shallots, finely chopped
1 tablespoon olive oil
2 tablespoons flour
½ cup port
1 cup milk
1 cup chicken stock

4 ounces Stilton, crumbled
2 teaspoons Dijon mustard
⅛ teaspoon white pepper
8 ounces macaroni, cooked
¼ cup bread crumbs
1 teaspoon paprika

Sauté the shallots in the oil in a skillet for 2 minutes. Sprinkle the flour over the shallots. Cook for 2 minutes, stirring occasionally. Pour in the port, milk and stock, whisking constantly. Bring to a simmer. Simmer for 3 minutes. Stir in 2 ounces of the Stilton, mustard and pepper. Cook until the cheese has melted, stirring constantly. Stir in the macaroni.

Spoon the macaroni mixture into an 8-inch-square baking dish. Combine the remaining Stilton and the bread crumbs in a bowl and mix well. Sprinkle over the macaroni mixture. Garnish with the paprika. Bake in a preheated 350-degree oven for 20 to 25 minutes or until bubbly and crisp.

Yield: 6 servings

Pasta with Summer Vegetable Ragout

2 cups chopped eggplant
2 sprigs fresh rosemary
¼ cup olive oil
1 cup thinly sliced red onion
6 cloves of garlic, crushed
1 red bell pepper, seeded, sliced
1 yellow bell pepper, seeded,
    sliced
1 cup chopped yellow squash

1 cup chopped zucchini
1 tablespoon fresh thyme
1 tablespoon freshly grated
    orange rind
2 cups chopped seeded ripe
    tomatoes
¼ cup balsamic vinegar
Salt and pepper to taste
10 ounces penne or ziti pasta

Sauté the eggplant and rosemary in the oil in a skillet for 5 minutes.

Add the onion and garlic. Sauté until the onion is translucent.

Add the red pepper and yellow pepper to the skillet. Sauté until the
peppers are tender-crisp.

Add the squash and zucchini. Reduce the heat. Cook for 4 to 5 minutes.

Stir in the thyme, grated orange rind, tomatoes and vinegar. Cook for
5 minutes. Season with salt and pepper. Remove from heat. Cover to
keep warm.

Cook the pasta using the package directions; drain.

Combine the pasta and the vegetable mixture in a bowl and toss to coat.
May be served hot or cold.

Yield: 4 servings

Star Spangled Pasta

1½ pounds fresh tomatoes
½ cup olive oil
2 tablespoons red wine
   vinegar
1 teaspoon salt
2 cloves of garlic, minced

1 or 2 fresh jalapeños, seeded,
   minced
6 ounces Monterey Jack cheese,
   finely chopped
¼ cup chopped cilantro
1 pound penne or ziti pasta

Core, seed and coarsely chop the tomatoes. Combine the tomatoes, oil, vinegar, salt, garlic, jalapeños and cheese in a bowl and mix well. Stir in the cilantro.

Cook the pasta using the package directions; drain.

Add the tomato mixture to the hot pasta and toss to coat.

Variation: May substitute 1 tablespoon dried cilantro plus 3 tablespoons chopped parsley for the ¼ cup chopped cilantro.

Yield: 4 servings

Fresh Vegetable Linguine

2 medium zucchini, sliced
2 medium yellow squash, sliced
1 cup broccoli
½ cup sliced onion
1 cup chopped red bell pepper
1 cup sliced mushrooms

12 ounces linguine
½ cup butter or margarine,
   melted
½ cup whipping cream
¾ cup grated Parmesan cheese
Freshly ground pepper

Steam the zucchini, squash, broccoli, onion and red pepper in a steamer for 5 to 7 minutes or until tender-crisp. Add the mushrooms. Steam for 1 minute; drain.

Cook the linguine in boiling salted water in a saucepan using the package directions; drain. Combine the linguine, butter, cream, cheese and pepper in a large bowl and mix well. Add the vegetables and toss to mix.

Yield: 8 servings

Complements

FRESH SAVORY ADDITIONS

"I don't like what passes for music today. Maybe I'm old-fashioned. I like something with a tune or melody to it."

*I*n 1934, Judge Truman exchanged his title for Senator Truman, winning his first statewide election by 262,000 votes. He was reelected in 1940 and soon began gaining national notoriety by heading a committee that investigated excessive spending and waste in defense operations. Total savings from the Truman Committee's work have been estimated to be as high as $4 billion to $6 billion. The Committee's success brought Truman an offer of $50,000 for a series of lectures, which he declined. He was not the kind of man to cash in on power or position.

At the Democratic Convention in 1944, it was commonly viewed that the party was not nominating a president and a vice president, but rather two presidents, as Roosevelt's failing health was widely known. After a wild ride of rumors and innuendos that had other nominees as shoo-ins, Truman was ultimately nominated as vice president. Truman expressed mixed emotions and Bess was dismayed about the nomination. Margaret recalled their ride home to Independence as "close to arctic."

Truman would serve as vice president for only 82 days before President Roosevelt died of a cerebral hemorrhage. He was initially overwhelmed by the enormity of his inherited responsibility and told a crowd of reporters, "Boys, if you ever pray, pray for me now. I don't know whether you fellows ever had a load of hay fall on you, but when they told me yesterday what had happened, I felt like the moon, the stars and all the planets had fallen on me."

Green Vegetable Medley

1 small leek
1 bunch spinach
1 teaspoon salt
1 bunch asparagus, ends trimmed

1 tablespoon unsalted butter
4 ounces sweet baby peas
Freshly ground pepper to taste

Trim the dark green leaves from the leek. Cut the leek into ¼-inch-thick slices. Rinse and pat dry.

Rinse the spinach and pat dry. Remove the stems.

Bring enough water to cover the asparagus to a boil in a medium skillet. Add ½ teaspoon of the salt. Add the asparagus. Simmer, covered, for 4 minutes or until tender-crisp; drain. Divide the asparagus among 4 serving plates.

Melt the butter in the skillet. Add the leek and cook for 2 minutes or until tender.

Add the spinach, peas, remaining ½ teaspoon salt and pepper and mix well.

Cook, covered, for 3 minutes or until the spinach is wilted and the peas are tender-crisp. Spoon over the asparagus.

Yield: 4 servings

Bleu Cheese Green Beans

2 ounces bleu cheese, crumbled
3 tablespoons half-and-half
2 tablespoons white wine vinegar
1 tablespoon grated Parmesan
 cheese
½ teaspoon oregano
¼ teaspoon pepper
⅛ teaspoon sugar

¼ cup vegetable oil
1 pound fresh or frozen green
 beans
¼ teaspoon salt
Pepper to taste
4 slices bacon, crisp-fried,
 crumbled

Combine 1 ounce of the bleu cheese, half-and-half, vinegar, Parmesan cheese, oregano, pepper and sugar in a blender container. Process until smooth. Add the oil in a stream, processing constantly at high speed.

Rinse and trim the beans. Bring enough water to cover the beans to a boil in a saucepan. Add the beans. Cook until tender-crisp; drain.

Place beans in a serving bowl. Sprinkle with salt and pepper.

Pour the bleu cheese sauce over the beans. Sprinkle with the remaining 1 ounce of blue cheese and the bacon.

Yield: 4 servings

Green Bean Pepper Parmesan

1 tablespoon canola oil
2 tablespoons water
1 medium yellow bell pepper,
*   seeded, chopped*
¼ cup chopped onion
½ teaspoon minced garlic

1 pound fresh green beans,
*   trimmed, cut into 1-inch pieces*
1 teaspoon dried basil
¼ teaspoon salt
½ cup grated Parmesan cheese

Heat the oil over medium heat in a large heavy skillet. Add the water, bell pepper, onion and garlic.

Cook for 3 minutes or until the onion is tender, stirring occasionally.

Add the beans, basil and salt and mix well. Cook, covered, until the beans are tender-crisp. Remove from heat. Stir in ¼ cup of the Parmesan cheese.

Spoon the bean mixture into a serving bowl. Sprinkle with the remaining ¼ cup Parmesan cheese.

Yield: 6 servings

★ ★ ★ ★ ★

Sweet and Sour Beans

1 pound green beans
1½ teaspoons cornstarch
1 cup chicken broth
2 tablespoons butter

½ teaspoon Dijon mustard
2 tablespoons brown sugar
2 tablespoons cider vinegar

Rinse and trim the beans. Cut the beans into 1-inch pieces.

Bring enough water to cover the beans to a boil in a saucepan. Add the beans. Cook until tender-crisp; drain. Rinse with cold water; drain.

Combine the cornstarch with a small amount of the broth and mix well.

Melt the butter in a large saucepan. Stir in the mustard, brown sugar and vinegar. Cook for 30 seconds, stirring constantly. Stir in the remaining chicken broth. Add the cornstarch mixture.

Cook until the sauce is clear and of the desired consistency, stirring constantly.

Add the beans. Cook until heated through.

Yield: 4 servings

Tangy Green Beans

12 ounces fresh green beans
2 tablespoons water
2 tablespoons butter

⅓ cup chopped walnuts or
   pecans
½ cup crumbled feta cheese

Rinse and trim the beans. Place the beans and water in a microwave-safe dish. Microwave on High for 12 minutes or until the beans are tender-crisp.

Combine the butter and walnuts in a small microwave-safe dish. Microwave on High for 2 minutes.

Stir the walnut mixture into the beans. Sprinkle with the cheese.

Yield: 4 servings

Hawaiian Vegetables

2 cups (2-inch-long) carrot strips
1 cup coarsely chopped celery
1 cup coarsely chopped green bell
  pepper
1 yellow onion, coarsely chopped
1 (8-ounce) can pineapple chunks
1 tablespoon margarine

¼ cup (scant) packed brown
  sugar
½ teaspoon salt
1 (8-ounce) can sliced water
  chestnuts
1½ tablespoons cornstarch

Bring enough water to cover the vegetables to a boil in a saucepan. Add the carrots, celery, green pepper and onion. Parboil; drain.

Drain the pineapple, reserving the juice. Melt the margarine in a saucepan. Stir in the brown sugar. Add the cooked vegetables. Cook for 4 minutes, stirring frequently. Add the reserved pineapple juice and salt. Bring to a simmer. Simmer for 3 minutes. Stir in the pineapple and water chestnuts. Simmer for 1 minute or until vegetables are tender-crisp.

Dissolve the cornstarch in ½ cup water in a small bowl. Stir into the vegetable mixture. Cook over medium heat until the sauce is clear and of the desired consistency, stirring constantly.

Yield: 8 servings

Baked Chile-Cheese Corn

8 ounces cream cheese, softened
2 teaspoons chili powder
2 teaspoons ground cumin
1 cup shredded Cheddar cheese

1 (4-ounce) can green chiles
4 cups frozen corn, thawed,
    drained

Combine the cream cheese, chili powder and cumin in a bowl and mix well.

Stir in the Cheddar cheese, chiles and corn. Pour into a greased 1½-quart baking dish.

Bake at 350 degrees for 30 minutes.

Yield: 6 servings

Golden Potatoes

4 (4-inch-long) Idaho potatoes
¼ cup butter
½ teaspoon salt
¼ teaspoon garlic powder
⅓ cup milk
3 ounces cream cheese, softened
2 tablespoons minced green
    onions

2 tablespoons minced fresh
    parsley
1 cup shredded sharp Cheddar
    cheese
¼ teaspoon paprika

Bake the potatoes at 400 degrees for 1 hour. Cut each potato in half lengthwise. Scoop out the potato, reserving the shells. Beat the potato, butter, salt, garlic powder and milk in a bowl until fluffy. Fold in the cream cheese, green onions and parsley.

Spoon the potato mixture into the reserved shells. Place the shells on a baking sheet. Sprinkle the Cheddar cheese over the potato mixture. Garnish with the paprika. Bake at 350 degrees for 30 minutes.

Yield: 8 servings

Dijon Potatoes

3 large potatoes, peeled, cut into
    ½-inch slices
1 tablespoon unsalted butter
½ cup finely chopped onions
2 cloves of garlic, minced
2 tablespoons flour
1 cup low-fat milk

2 tablespoons salt-free Dijon
    mustard
¼ cup finely chopped parsley
Pepper to taste
¼ cup whole wheat bread
    crumbs

Place the potatoes in water to cover in a saucepan. Bring to a boil. Boil for 5 to 8 minutes or just until tender; drain.

Melt the butter in a skillet over medium heat. Add the onions and garlic. Cook for 5 minutes, stirring constantly.

Add the flour. Cook for 3 to 4 minutes, stirring constantly.

Stir in the milk gradually. Bring to a boil, stirring constantly. Boil until of the desired consistency. Reduce the heat to low.

Cook for 10 minutes. Stir in the mustard, parsley and pepper.

Arrange the potato slices in the bottom of a shallow baking dish. Pour the sauce over the potatoes. Sprinkle with the bread crumbs.

Bake at 350 degrees for 15 minutes.

Yield: 6 servings

Potato Gratin

2 large potatoes
2 sweet potatoes
1 tablespoon minced fresh
   rosemary
Salt and pepper to taste

1½ cups heavy cream
1 cup shredded Gruyère or aged
   Swiss cheese
½ cup grated Parmesan cheese

Cut the potatoes and sweet potatoes into thin slices.

Alternate layers of the potatoes and sweet potatoes, sprinkling the rosemary, salt and pepper between each layer in a microwave-safe gratin dish. Pour the cream over the layers.

Microwave, covered, on High for 15 minutes. Sprinkle the Gruyère and Parmesan cheeses over the top.

Microwave on High for 5 minutes or until the cheese is bubbly.

Variations: May substitute 2 teaspoons dried crumbled rosemary for the fresh rosemary. May bake at 350 degrees for 35 minutes. Sprinkle the Gruyère and Parmesan cheeses over the top. Broil for 3 to 5 minutes or until the cheese is golden and bubbly.

Yield: 8 servings

★　　　★　　　★　　　★　　　★

Swiss Potato Gratin

3 pounds potatoes, such as Yukon Gold
2½ teaspoons dried sage
Salt and pepper to taste

6 ounces Swiss cheese, shredded
1 cup heavy cream
1 cup dry white wine

Scrub the potatoes. Cut into ¼-inch slices.

Layer the potatoes, sage, salt, pepper and cheese ⅓ at a time in a greased 9x13-inch baking pan.

Whisk the cream and white wine in a bowl. Pour over the layers.

Bake at 400 degrees for 50 minutes or until the potatoes are tender.

Yield: 6 servings

"My home town, Independence, the County Seat of Jackson County, Missouri, is in my opinion the best place for a retired Missouri farmer to live. That state has had three 'notorious' characters—Mark Twain, Jesse James and myself. The other two are shoveling coal for Pluto and I'm all that's left to appear for them."

Ratatouille

1 medium eggplant, or 2 small
* eggplants*
2 teaspoons salt
¼ cup olive oil
1 large red or white onion, sliced
4 cloves of garlic, minced
1 green bell pepper, seeded, cut
* into strips*

1 red bell pepper, seeded, cut into
* strips*
2 zucchini, chopped
5 tomatoes, cut into wedges
1 bay leaf

Cut the eggplant into ½-inch cubes. Place the eggplant in a shallow dish. Sprinkle with the salt. Let stand for 15 minutes or longer to drain. Pat firmly with paper towels to dry.

Heat the oil in a large skillet. Add the onion, garlic, green pepper and red pepper. Cook for 2 minutes.

Add the eggplant. Cook over high heat for 3 minutes or until lightly browned.

Add the zucchini, tomatoes and bay leaf. Reduce the heat to low. Simmer, covered, for 30 minutes. Cook, uncovered, over medium heat for 10 minutes or until most of the liquid has evaporated.

Discard the bay leaf. Garnish with finely chopped parsley. May be served hot or at room temperature.

Variation: Serve over rice as a main dish.

Yield: 6 servings

Roasted Roots

1 pound small red potatoes,
  peeled
1 (8- to 12-ounce) piece celery
  root, peeled
1½ teaspoons salt
1 pound carrots, peeled
3 medium parsnips, peeled
5 tablespoons extra-virgin
  olive oil

1 head of garlic, separated into
  cloves
2 tablespoons balsamic or red
  wine vinegar
1 teaspoon (heaping) mild
  paprika
1½ teaspoons coriander seeds,
  crushed
Freshly ground pepper

Cut the potatoes and celery root into equal-sized pieces. Combine 1 teaspoon of the salt, potatoes and celery root with enough water to cover in a saucepan. Bring to a boil. Simmer for 5 minutes. Drain, reserving 5 tablespoons of the water.

Cut the carrots and parsnips into wedges.

Pour the oil into a large baking dish. Place in the oven and heat.

Place the potatoes, celery root, carrots and parsnips in the baking dish, stirring to coat.

Combine the vinegar, paprika, coriander seeds and reserved water in a small bowl and mix well. Stir in the remaining ½ teaspoon of salt and pepper. Pour over the vegetables.

Bake in a preheated 400-degree oven for 1 hour and 15 minutes or until tender and browned, turning 2 or 3 times. Sprinkle with coarsely ground salt before serving.

Yield: 8 servings

Red Tape Rhubarb

½ cup butter, melted
1 cup sugar
3 cups dried bread cubes

4 to 5 cups sliced rhubarb
(about 1¼ pounds)

Combine the butter and sugar in a bowl and mix well.

Add the bread cubes. Toss to coat. Stir in the rhubarb. Spoon into a 9x9-inch baking pan.

Bake at 350 degrees for 45 minutes or until the rhubarb is tender.

Yield: 6 servings

Hearty Sweet Potatoes

3 cups mashed cooked peeled
sweet potatoes
½ cup butter, melted
2 eggs, beaten
1 teaspoon cinnamon
¾ cup sugar

1 teaspoon vanilla extract
¼ cup butter
1 tablespoon flour
¾ cup packed brown sugar
1 cup chopped pecans

Combine the sweet potatoes, melted butter, eggs, cinnamon, granulated sugar and vanilla in a bowl and mix well.

Pour into a buttered 9-inch square baking pan.

Combine the ¼ cup butter, flour, brown sugar and pecans in a bowl and mix well.

Sprinkle the pecan mixture over the potato mixture.

Bake at 325 degrees for 35 minutes.

Yield: 6 servings

Summer Tomato Basil Tart

4 large tomatoes, cut into
¼-inch-thick slices
Salt
1 cup firmly packed basil leaves
½ cup plus 2 tablespoons ricotta
cheese
2 eggs

4 ounces mozzarella cheese,
shredded
½ cup grated Parmesan cheese
1½ teaspoons salt
Pepper to taste
Bacon Pastry Shell, baked
1 teaspoon vegetable oil

Lightly salt the tomatoes on both sides. Drain on paper towels.

Purée the basil and ricotta in a blender. Add the eggs. Process until smooth. Combine the basil mixture, mozzarella cheese, Parmesan cheese, the 1½ teaspoons salt and pepper in a bowl and mix well.

Arrange the tomato end slices in the bottom of the Bacon Pastry Shell. Spoon the cheese mixture over the tomatoes. Arrange the remaining tomatoes over the cheese mixture. Brush with the oil.

Bake in a preheated 350-degree oven for 40 to 50 minutes or until set. Cool on a wire rack for 10 minutes.

Bacon Pastry Shell

1¼ cups flour
4 ounces bacon, crisp-fried,
crumbled
¼ teaspoon salt

6 tablespoons unsalted butter
2 tablespoons cold vegetable
shortening
3 to 4 tablespoons ice water

Combine the flour, bacon and salt in a large bowl and mix well. Cut in the butter and shortening until crumbly. Add the water 1 tablespoon at a time, mixing with a fork until the flour mixture forms a ball. Chill, wrapped in plastic wrap, for 1 hour or longer.

Roll the dough into a 12-inch circle on a lightly floured surface. Fit into a 9-inch tart pan. Prick the shell with a fork. Chill, covered, for 30 minutes. Line the shell with foil. Fill with rice. Bake in a preheated 425-degree oven for 15 minutes. Remove the rice and foil. Bake for 3 to 5 minutes longer or until golden brown.

Yield: 6 servings

★ ★ ★ ★ ★

Vegetable Frittata

3 cloves of garlic, minced
1 red onion, sliced
2 red bell peppers, seeded,
*   thinly sliced*
1 yellow bell pepper, seeded,
*   thinly sliced*
3 tablespoons olive oil
2 yellow squash, thinly sliced
2 zucchini, thinly sliced

8 ounces mushrooms, sliced
6 eggs
¼ cup whipping cream
2 teaspoons salt
2 teaspoons pepper
8 slices bread, cubed
8 ounces cream cheese, cubed
8 ounces Swiss cheese, shredded

Sauté the garlic, onion, red peppers and yellow pepper in 1 tablespoon of the oil in a skillet until tender-crisp. Drain and pat dry.

Sauté the squash and zucchini in 1 tablespoon of the oil in a skillet until tender-crisp. Drain and pat dry.

Sauté the mushrooms in the remaining 1 tablespoon oil until tender. Drain and pat dry.

Whisk the eggs, whipping cream, salt and pepper in a bowl. Stir in the sautéed vegetables, half the bread cubes, cream cheese and Swiss cheese.

Press the remaining bread cubes in the bottom of a lightly greased 10-inch springform pan. Place the pan on a baking sheet. Spoon the vegetable mixture into the pan.

Bake at 325 degrees for 45 minutes. Cover with foil. Bake for 15 minutes longer.

Yield: 8 servings

Zorba's Zucchini

1 tablespoon olive oil
½ cup chopped onions
3 cloves of garlic, minced
2 teaspoons dried oregano
3 cups zucchini, cut into ½-inch
slices
1 cup chopped tomatoes

½ teaspoon freshly ground
pepper
¼ cup chopped pitted Kalamata
olives
8 ounces feta cheese, crumbled
¼ cup seasoned bread crumbs

Heat the oil in a nonstick skillet over medium heat. Add the onions, garlic and oregano. Sauté for 2 minutes or until tender.

Add the zucchini. Sauté for 1 minute.

Stir in the tomatoes, pepper and olives. Remove from heat. Pour into a 1½-quart baking dish.

Combine the cheese and bread crumbs in a bowl. Sprinkle over the zucchini mixture.

Bake at 350 degrees for 10 minutes or until the top is golden brown and the vegetables are tender.

Yield: 4 servings

Herb Butters

¼ pound butter, softened
1 tablespoon lemon juice
3 tablespoons finely chopped
fresh parsley

Salt and freshly ground pepper
to taste

Cream the butter in a mixer bowl until fluffy. Beat in the lemon juice gradually. Add the parsley, salt and pepper and mix well.

Chill, wrapped in plastic wrap, until firm.

Variation: May substitute fresh tarragon or rosemary for the parsley or 3 teaspoons dried parsley for the fresh parsley.

Yield: 8 (1-tablespoon) servings

Herbed Caper Butter

4 tablespoons butter
2 teaspoons capers

½ teaspoon oregano
Freshly ground pepper to taste

Combine the butter, capers, oregano and pepper in a saucepan. Heat until the butter is melted, stirring constantly.

Serve over cooked vegetables.

Yield: 4 (1-tablespoon) servings

Red Wine Butter for Steak

2 teaspoons minced shallots
1 clove of garlic, minced
1 cup plus 2 tablespoons dry red
  wine
1 teaspoon chopped parsley

4 to 5 tablespoons butter,
  softened
Salt and freshly ground pepper
  to taste

Combine the shallots, garlic and wine in a saucepan and mix well. Cook until the liquid has been reduced to one-fourth of the original amount. Remove from heat. Let stand until cooled.

Cream the parsley and butter in a mixer bowl until fluffy. Beat in the wine mixture, salt and pepper.

Chill, wrapped in plastic wrap, until firm. Serve on top of hot broiled or grilled meat.

Yield: 4 servings

Portobello Mushroom Sauce

½ large or 1 small onion,
  chopped
1 clove of garlic, minced
⅓ cup virgin olive oil
1 large portobello mushroom,
  sliced

½ teaspoon salt
1 teaspoon black pepper
½ teaspoon red pepper
¾ cup white wine
1 tablespoon cornstarch
2 teaspoons fresh chopped parsley

Sauté the onion and garlic in the olive oil in a skillet until the onion is browned. Add the mushroom, salt, black pepper and red pepper. Sauté until the mushroom is tender.

Add the wine. Simmer over low heat until the wine is absorbed. Stir in the cornstarch. Cook until of the desired consistency, stirring occasionally. Remove from heat.

Stir in the parsley. Serve over polenta or red meat.

Yield: 4 servings

Sweet and Spicy Couscous

1¼ cups couscous
1½ cups chicken broth
1 red onion, chopped
1 red bell pepper, seeded, chopped
2 tablespoons olive oil
1 zucchini, chopped

1 yellow squash, chopped
1 cup golden raisins
½ to 1 teaspoon cumin
½ to 1 teaspoon curry
Dash of red pepper flakes
Butter to taste

Prepare the couscous in a saucepan using the package directions and substituting chicken broth for the water. Set aside.

Sauté the onion and red bell pepper in the oil in a skillet for 5 minutes.

Add the zucchini and squash. Sauté until tender-crisp. Remove from heat. Stir in the raisins, cumin, curry and red pepper flakes.

Add the onion mixture to the couscous and mix well.

Spoon into a baking dish. Dot the top with butter.

Bake at 350 degrees for 15 to 20 minutes or until the top is golden. Garnish with plain nonfat yogurt.

Yield: 4 servings

Baked Grits

1½ cups grits
5 cups water
Salt to taste
1 cup butter
16 ounces Cheddar cheese

3 eggs, beaten
1 tablespoon savory salt
2 teaspoons paprika
Dash of Tabasco sauce

Combine the grits, water and salt in a saucepan and mix well. Cook until of the desired consistency, stirring occasionally.

Cut the butter into small pieces. Cut the cheese into small pieces.

Add the butter, cheese, eggs, savory salt, paprika and Tabasco to the cooked grits.

Cook until the butter and cheese are melted, stirring constantly. Spoon into a baking dish.

Bake at 350 degrees for 40 minutes.

Yield: 12 servings

Orzo and Rice Pilaf

1 tablespoon margarine or butter
¼ cup orzo
1 very small onion, finely
   chopped

¾ cup long grain rice
⅛ teaspoon coarsely ground
   pepper
1 (14-ounce) can chicken broth

Melt the margarine in a 2-quart saucepan over medium-high heat. Stir in the orzo. Cook until the orzo is browned, stirring occasionally.

Add the onion. Cook for 5 minutes or until the onion is tender.

Add the rice and pepper, stirring to coat.

Add the broth. Bring to a boil. Reduce heat to low. Simmer, covered, for 18 to 20 minutes or until the orzo and rice are tender and the liquid is absorbed.

Yield: 4 servings

DBS Wild Rice

1 cup wild rice
¼ cup butter
½ cup slivered almonds
2 tablespoons finely chopped
   onion

8 ounces fresh mushrooms, sliced
1 teaspoon salt
3 cups chicken or beef broth

Bring 2 cups of water to a boil. Remove from heat. Add the rice. Let stand for 30 minutes; drain. Repeat the process.

Melt the butter in a heavy skillet. Stir in the rice, almonds, onion, mushrooms and salt. Sauté for 5 minutes; do not brown.

Spoon into a buttered 2½-quart baking dish. Pour the broth over the rice mixture.

Bake, covered, at 325 degrees for 1 hour. Bake, uncovered, for 15 minutes or until the liquid is absorbed.

Yield: 4 servings

★　　★　　★　　★　　★

Temptations

ULTIMATE ENDINGS & CELEBRATIONS

*"It is remarkable indeed how time flies and makes you
an old man whether you want to be or not."*

★　　★　　★　　★　　★

★　　★　　★　　★　　★

Although Harry Truman is credited with many decisions involving war issues, his primary focus was peace. He was responsible for redesigning the Presidential Seal, so the eagle would face the olive branch rather than the cluster of arrows. He is widely regarded as a benchmark for integrity. He brought his Midwestern common sense, absolute honesty, and deep respect for and knowledge of history to the office of the presidency. These qualities served him well in the monumental decisions he faced as president from 1945 to 1952.

Harry Truman retired to Independence in 1953 and helped establish the Truman Library in 1957. It was not uncommon to see him on his daily walks around town. He said, "I like to stop and talk with people. I like to know what's going on in the town and understand what my neighbors are doing. I have a good time. In Independence, I usually walk when it's too early for many people to be out — about six or six-thirty. It's not done to avoid anyone but to be able to get in a good day's work." He worked six and one-half days each week for nine years at the library, longer than his term as president.

Harry Truman died on December 26, 1972, at the age of 88. He and Bess are buried in the courtyard of the Truman Library in Independence, Missouri.

★　　★　　★　　★　　★

Harry T's Apple Cake

2 eggs
2 cups sugar
2 teaspoons cinnamon
½ cup vegetable oil
2 cups flour

⅛ teaspoon salt
2 teaspoons baking soda
4 cups chopped apples
1 cup chopped walnuts or pecans
Cream Cheese Icing

Combine the eggs, sugar, cinnamon and oil in a mixer bowl and mix well.

Sift the flour, salt and baking soda together. Add to the sugar mixture and mix well. Beat at high speed for 4 minutes or until smooth and creamy. Stir in the apples and walnuts.

Spoon into a greased and floured bundt pan.

Bake at 350 degrees for 40 to 45 minutes or until the cake tests done. Cool in the pan for 10 minutes. Invert onto a serving plate.

Spread the Cream Cheese Icing over the cooled cake.

Cream Cheese Icing

½ cup butter, softened
3 ounces cream cheese, softened
1 teaspoon vanilla extract

4 cups (about) confectioners'
    sugar

Beat the butter and cream cheese in a mixer bowl until creamy. Add the vanilla and mix well. Beat in the confectioners' sugar gradually until of spreading consistency.

Yield: 16 servings

Wacky Chocolate Cake

1½ cups flour
1 cup sugar
1 teaspoon baking soda
3 tablespoons baking cocoa
¼ teaspoon salt
1 teaspoon vanilla extract

1 teaspoon vinegar
5 tablespoons vegetable oil
1 cup water
The Very Best Homemade Ice
  Cream

Combine the flour, sugar, baking soda, baking cocoa, salt, vanilla, vinegar, oil and water in a bowl and mix well with a spoon.

Pour into a greased and floured 9x13-inch cake pan.

Bake at 350 degrees for 25 to 30 minutes or until a wooden pick inserted in the center comes out clean. Serve with The Very Best Homemade Ice Cream.

Yield: 15 servings

The Very Best Homemade Ice Cream

4 eggs
2 cups sugar
½ teaspoon salt

3 cups whipping cream
1 tablespoon vanilla extract
8 cups milk

Beat the eggs in a large bowl until light and fluffy. Add the sugar and salt gradually, beating well. Add the whipping cream and vanilla and mix well. Add the milk and mix well. Pour into the ice cream freezer.

Freeze according to manufacturer's directions.

Yield: 20 servings

Black Pepper Pound Cake

1 cup butter, softened
1 cup sugar
4 eggs
1½ cups flour
¼ teaspoon salt

½ teaspoon cream of tartar
¾ teaspoon freshly ground pepper
1 tablespoon lemon juice
1 teaspoon vanilla extract
Bourbon Sauce

Beat the butter in a large mixer bowl until creamy. Add the sugar gradually. Beat for 5 to 7 minutes or until light and fluffy. Add the eggs 1 at a time, mixing well after each addition.

Combine the flour, salt, cream of tartar and pepper in a bowl and mix well. Add to the butter mixture gradually. Beat at low speed just until blended. Stir in the lemon juice and vanilla.

Pour into a greased and floured bundt pan.

Bake in a preheated 325-degree oven for 50 to 55 minutes or until the cake tests done. Cool on a wire rack for 10 to 15 minutes. Invert onto a serving plate. Serve with Bourbon Sauce.

Bourbon Sauce

¾ cup packed light brown sugar
½ cup butter

½ cup half-and-half
1 to 2 tablespoons bourbon

Heat the brown sugar, butter and half-and-half in a saucepan over low heat until the sugar dissolves and the butter is melted, stirring occasionally. Remove from heat.

Stir in the bourbon. Serve warm.

Yield: 16 servings

Butternut Pound Cake

1 cup butter or margarine,
  softened
½ cup shortening
3 cups sugar
5 eggs

1 (5-ounce) can evaporated milk
3¼ cups flour
¼ teaspoon salt
2 tablespoons butternut flavoring
Creamy Caramel Sauce

Cream the butter and shortening in a mixer bowl until light and fluffy. Add the sugar gradually, beating for 5 to 7 minutes. Add the eggs one at a time, mixing well after each addition.

Pour the evaporated milk into a 1-cup measure. Add enough water to measure 1 cup. Combine the flour and salt in a bowl and mix well. Add the flour mixture and milk mixture alternately to the creamed mixture, mixing well after each addition. Stir in the flavoring. Pour into a greased and floured 10-inch tube pan.

Bake at 325 degrees for 1 hour and 25 minutes or until a wooden pick inserted in the center comes out clean. Cool in the pan for 10 to 15 minutes. Invert onto a wire rack to cool completely. Serve with Creamy Caramel Sauce.

Creamy Caramel Sauce

1 cup firmly packed brown sugar
1 cup whipping cream

1 cup half-and-half
3 tablespoons butter

Combine the brown sugar, whipping cream, half-and-half and butter in a heavy saucepan and mix well. Cook over low heat for 45 minutes or until of the desired consistency, stirring occasionally. Serve warm.

Yield: 16 servings

Hershey's Pound Cake

1 cup butter	*2½ cups cake flour*
2 cups sugar	*¼ teaspoon salt*
4 eggs	*½ teaspoon baking soda*
¾ cup Hershey's syrup	*1 cup buttermilk*
7 (7-ounce) Hershey's candy bars	*2 teaspoons vanilla extract*

Cream the butter and sugar in a mixer bowl until light and fluffy. Add the eggs 1 at a time, mixing well after each addition.

Heat the syrup in a saucepan. Add the candy bars. Cook until the candy bars are melted, stirring occasionally.

Add to the creamed mixture alternately with the flour, mixing well after each addition.

Dissolve the salt and baking soda in the buttermilk in a bowl. Stir into the batter. Add the vanilla and mix well. Pour into a greased tube pan.

Bake at 350 degrees for 1 hour or until the cake tests done. Cool in the pan for 10 minutes. Invert onto a wire rack to cool completely. Sprinkle with confectioners' sugar. Wrap in foil until ready to serve.

Yield: 16 servings

Chocolate Praline Cake

½ cup margarine
2 cups whipping cream
1 cup packed brown sugar
¾ cup chopped pecans
1 (2-layer) package devil's food
  chocolate cake mix

1¼ cups water
⅓ cup oil
3 eggs
¼ cup confectioners' sugar
¼ teaspoon vanilla extract

Combine the margarine, ¼ cup of the cream and the brown sugar in a saucepan. Cook over low heat until the margarine is melted, stirring occasionally. Pour into two 9-inch round cake pans. Sprinkle evenly with pecans.

Combine the cake mix, water, oil and eggs in a mixer bowl. Beat on high speed for 2 minutes. Spoon the batter over the pecans.

Bake at 325 degrees for 40 minutes or until the cake tests done. Cool in the pan for 5 minutes. Remove to a wire rack to cool completely.

Beat the remaining 1¾ cups cream in a small mixer bowl until soft peaks form. Add the confectioners' sugar and vanilla, beating until stiff peaks form.

Place 1 layer of the cake pecan side up on a serving plate. Spread half the whipped cream mixture over the layer. Place the remaining cake layer pecan side up over the whipped cream mixture. Spread the remaining whipped cream mixture over the cake.

Store, covered, in the refrigerator until ready to serve.

Yield: 14 servings

Pumpkin Gingerbread with Caramel Sauce

2¼ cups flour
½ cup sugar
⅔ cup butter or margarine
¾ cup chopped pecans
1½ teaspoons ginger
1 teaspoon baking soda
½ teaspoon cinnamon

¼ teaspoon salt
¼ teaspoon ground cloves
¾ cup buttermilk
½ cup light molasses
½ cup canned pumpkin
1 egg
Caramel Sauce

Combine the flour and sugar in a large bowl. Cut in the butter until the mixture resembles fine crumbs. Stir in the pecans. Press 1¼ cups of the crumb mixture into a 9x9-inch baking pan.

Add the ginger, baking soda, cinnamon, salt, cloves, buttermilk, molasses, pumpkin and egg to the remaining crumb mixture and mix well. Pour over the pressed crumb layer.

Bake at 350 degrees for 45 minutes or until a wooden pick inserted in the center comes out clean. Serve warm with Caramel Sauce.

Caramel Sauce

½ cup butter or margarine
1¼ cups packed brown sugar

2 tablespoons light corn syrup
½ cup whipping cream

Melt the butter in a saucepan. Stir in the brown sugar and corn syrup. Bring to a boil, stirring constantly.

Boil for 1 minute, stirring constantly. Stir in the cream. Return to a boil. Remove from heat. Serve warm.

Yield: 9 servings

Whiskey Fudge Cake

1¼ *cups pastry or cake flour*
1 *teaspoon baking soda*
10½ *ounces bittersweet chocolate,*
   cut into small chunks
¾ *cup butter, room temperature*
1¼ *cups sugar*

4 *egg yolks*
⅓ *cup whiskey or brandy, warmed*
   slightly
1 *tablespoon vanilla extract*
4 *egg whites*

Line a baking sheet with parchment paper. Set a 2¼x8-inch cake ring on it. Wrap an 8-inch round piece of cardboard with foil. Set aside.

Sift the flour and baking soda together in a bowl.

Melt the chocolate in a double boiler over simmering water.

Cream the butter in a mixer bowl until light. Add 1 cup of the sugar gradually, beating until light and fluffy. Add the egg yolks 1 at a time, mixing well after each addition. Add the whiskey and vanilla and mix well.

Pour in the chocolate and mix well. Fold in half the flour mixture. Fold in the remaining flour mixture.

Beat the egg whites in a mixer bowl until soft peaks form. Add the remaining ¼ cup sugar gradually, beating until shiny and firm but not stiff. Stir ¼ of the egg whites into the batter. Fold in the remaining egg whites. Pour the batter into the prepared cake ring.

Bake in a preheated 350-degree oven for 1 hour. Invert immediately onto the foil-covered cardboard round. Run a sharp knife around the side of the cake, loosening the cake from the ring; do not remove the ring. Cool completely on a wire rack. Lift the ring carefully when cooled. Garnish with sifted confectioners' sugar.

Yield: 12 servings

Apple Surprise Cupcakes

1½ cups sugar
1 cup shortening
3 eggs
2 cups flour
1 teaspoon baking soda
1½ teaspoons salt
1 teaspoon nutmeg

2 teaspoons cinnamon
2 tablespoons lemon juice
5 cups finely chopped apples
8 ounces cream cheese, softened
⅓ cup sugar
¾ cup butterscotch chips
¼ cup chopped walnuts

Cream the 1½ cups sugar and shortening in a mixer bowl until light and fluffy. Add the eggs 1 at a time, mixing well after each addition.

Combine the flour, baking soda, 1 teaspoon of the salt, nutmeg and cinnamon in a bowl and mix well. Add to the creamed mixture and mix well.

Add the lemon juice and mix well. Stir in the apples.

Spoon into 24 paper-lined muffin cups.

Cream the cream cheese, the ⅓ cup sugar and the remaining ½ teaspoon salt in a mixer bowl until light and fluffy. Stir in the butterscotch chips and walnuts. Place 1 rounded teaspoonful on top of the batter in each muffin cup.

Bake at 350 degrees for 25 to 30 minutes or until the cupcake springs back when touched in the center.

Yield: 24 cupcakes

Bess' Signature Coconut Balls

⅔ cup sweetened condensed milk
⅛ teaspoon salt

1 teaspoon vanilla extract
¼ teaspoon almond extract
1½ cups coconut

Combine the condensed milk, salt, vanilla and almond extracts in a bowl and mix well. Stir in the coconut.

Shape into 18 balls. Place 2 inches apart on a greased cookie sheet.

Bake at 350 degrees for 15 minutes or until lightly browned.

Yield: 18 balls

Bess Truman

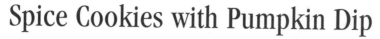

Spice Cookies with Pumpkin Dip

4 cups flour
4 teaspoons baking soda
2 teaspoons cinnamon
1 teaspoon ground ginger
1 teaspoon cloves
1 teaspoon salt

1½ cups butter or margarine
2 cups sugar
2 eggs
½ cup molasses
¼ cup sugar
Pumpkin Dip

Combine the flour, baking soda, cinnamon, ginger, cloves and salt in a bowl and mix well. Cream the butter and 2 cups sugar in a bowl until light and fluffy. Add the eggs and molasses and mix well. Add the dry ingredients and mix well. Chill, covered, for 8 to 12 hours or longer.

Shape into ½-inch balls. Roll in ¼ cup sugar. Place 2 inches apart on a greased cookie sheet. Bake at 375 degrees for 6 minutes or until cookies begin to brown. Serve with Pumpkin Dip.

Pumpkin Dip

1 (8-ounce) package cream
cheese, softened
1 (18-ounce) can pumpkin
pie mix

2 cups confectioners' sugar
½ to 1 teaspoon cinnamon
¼ to ½ teaspoon ground ginger

Combine the cream cheese, pumpkin pie mix, confectioners' sugar, cinnamon to taste and ginger to taste in a mixer bowl. Beat until smooth. Chill in refrigerator. Spoon into a serving bowl.

Yield: 24 servings

Coffee Iced Oatmeal Cookies

1 cup margarine
1 cup firmly packed brown sugar
1 cup granulated sugar
2 eggs
1½ cups flour

½ teaspoon salt
1 teaspoon baking soda
3 cups rolled oats
½ cup chopped pecans
Coffee Icing

Cream the margarine, brown sugar and granulated sugar in a mixer bowl until light and fluffy. Add the eggs 1 at a time, mixing well after each addition.

Combine the flour, salt and baking soda in a bowl and mix well. Beat into the creamed mixture. Stir in the oats and pecans.

Drop by teaspoonfuls 2 inches apart onto greased cookie sheets. Bake at 350 degrees for 10 minutes. Cool on a wire rack.

Frost the cooled cookies with Coffee Icing.

Coffee Icing

2 cups confectioners' sugar
2 teaspoons cinnamon
2 teaspoons vanilla extract

6 tablespoons melted butter
2 tablespoons very strong coffee

Combine the sugar, cinnamon, vanilla and butter in a bowl and mix well. Stir in the coffee gradually, mixing well after each addition.

Yield: 24 servings

Pecan Tea Cookies

1 cup butter
¾ cup sugar
1 tablespoon vinegar
1 teaspoon vanilla extract

1½ cups flour
½ teaspoon baking soda
1 cup chopped pecans

Cream the butter and sugar in a mixer bowl until light and fluffy. Add the vinegar and vanilla and mix well.

Combine the flour and baking soda in a bowl and mix well. Add to the creamed mixture and mix well. Stir in the pecans. Chill, covered, for 15 to 20 minutes.

Shape the dough by teaspoonfuls into small balls. Place 2 inches apart on greased cookie sheets. Flatten each ball with the bottom of a glass dipped in additional sugar. Bake at 300 degrees for 8 minutes or until golden.

Yield: 18 cookies

Disappearing Brownie Cookies

⅔ cup butter-flavor shortening
1½ cups firmly packed light
  brown sugar
1 tablespoon water
1 teaspoon vanilla extract
2 eggs

1½ cups flour
⅓ cup baking cocoa
¼ teaspoon baking soda
½ teaspoon salt
2 cups semisweet chocolate chips

Cream the shortening, brown sugar, water and vanilla in a mixer bowl until light and fluffy. Add the eggs 1 at a time, mixing well after each addition.

Combine the flour, baking cocoa, baking soda and salt in a bowl and mix well. Beat into the creamed mixture at low speed until well blended. Stir in the chocolate chips.

Drop by rounded tablespoonfuls 2 inches apart onto ungreased cookie sheets. Bake in a preheated 375-degree oven for 7 to 9 minutes; do not overbake.

Yield: 18 cookies

Choco-Sticks

2 ounces unsweetened chocolate
7 tablespoons butter
1 egg
½ cup sugar
¼ cup sifted flour

1 cup sifted confectioners' sugar
1 tablespoon whipping cream
½ teaspoon pure mint flavoring
Green food coloring

Combine 1 ounce of the chocolate and 4 tablespoons of the butter in the top of a double boiler over hot water. Cook until melted, stirring frequently. Cool slightly.

Beat the egg until frothy in a mixer bowl. Stir in the chocolate mixture. Add the sugar and mix well. Add the flour and mix well. Pour into a greased 8x8-inch baking pan.

Bake at 350 degrees for 15 to 20 minutes. Place on a wire rack to cool completely.

Combine 2 tablespoons of the butter, confectioners' sugar, cream and mint flavoring in a bowl and mix well. Stir in the food coloring until of the desired color. Spread over the baked layer. Chill for 10 minutes or longer.

Melt the remaining 1 ounce chocolate and the remaining 1 tablespoon butter in the top of a double boiler over hot water, stirring frequently. Pour over the chilled layers, tilting the pan to coat the top.

Chill, covered, for 15 minutes or until the chocolate coating hardens.

Cut into sixteen 1x4-inch sticks.

Yield: 16 servings

Oh Susannah Bars

½ cup melted butter or margarine
1 (2-layer) package yellow cake
 mix
3 eggs

8 ounces cream cheese, softened
1 pound confectioners' sugar
½ cup coconut
1 cup chopped pecans

Combine the butter, cake mix and 1 of the eggs in a bowl and mix well. Press into the bottom of a jelly roll pan.

Beat the remaining 2 eggs in a bowl. Add the cream cheese and beat until smooth. Add the confectioners' sugar and mix well. Stir in the coconut and pecans. Spoon over the pressed layer. Bake at 325 degrees for 45 minutes.

Yield: 16 bars

Red Raspberry and White Bars

1 cup butter
1 (10-ounce) package plus 1 cup
 vanilla milk chips
4 eggs
1 cup sugar

2 cups flour
1½ teaspoons almond extract
1 cup raspberry jam or
 spreadable fruit
½ cup sliced almonds, toasted

Heat the butter in a small saucepan over low heat until melted. Remove from heat. Add the package of vanilla milk chips; do not stir. Beat the eggs in a mixer bowl until foamy. Beat in the sugar gradually at high speed until mixture is pale yellow. Add the flour and mix well. Stir in the butter mixture. Stir in the almond extract. Spread half the batter in a greased and floured 9x13-inch baking pan.

Bake in a preheated 325-degree oven for 15 to 20 minutes or until golden brown. Melt the jam in a saucepan over low heat. Spread over the warm baked layer. Stir the remaining chips into the remaining batter. Drop by teaspoonfuls over the jam. Sprinkle with the almonds.

Bake for 25 to 30 minutes or until a wooden pick inserted in the center comes out clean. Cool completely. Cut into bars.

Yield: 15 bars

Tailgate Brownies

4 ounces semisweet chocolate
1 cup margarine
4 eggs
2 teaspoons vanilla extract

1 cup flour
1¾ cups sugar
2 to 3 cups chopped pecans

Combine the chocolate and margarine in a saucepan. Cook over low heat until melted, stirring frequently.

Add the eggs, vanilla, flour and sugar and stir 50 strokes. Stir in the desired amount of pecans.

Spoon the batter into 24 paper-lined muffin cups.

Bake at 350 degrees for 23 to 25 minutes or until the brownies pull away from the edge of the muffin cups; do not overbake.

Variation: May use 48 miniature muffin cups and bake for 18 to 20 minutes or until the brownies pull away from the edge.

Yield: 24 brownies

Show Me More Brownies

1 cup butter	3 cups quick-cooking oats
2 cups packed brown sugar	2 cups semisweet chocolate chips
2 eggs	1 (14-ounce) can sweetened
2 teaspoons vanilla extract	condensed milk
2½ cups flour	2 tablespoons butter
1 teaspoon baking soda	½ teaspoon salt
1 teaspoon salt	

Cream the butter and brown sugar in a mixer bowl until light and fluffy. Add the eggs and vanilla and mix well.

Sift the flour, baking soda and salt together. Add to the creamed mixture and mix well. Stir in the oats.

Spoon ⅔ of the batter into a greased 9x13-inch baking pan.

Combine the chocolate chips, condensed milk, butter and salt in a saucepan. Cook over low heat until the chocolate chips and butter are melted, stirring frequently. Spread over the batter. Spoon the remaining batter over the chocolate mixture.

Bake at 350 degrees for 30 minutes.

Yield: 15 brownies

Better Than Apple Pie

1 (15-ounce) package refrigerated	**4 cups chopped peeled apples**
pie pastry	**½ cup butter or margarine**
¾ cup sugar	**½ cup packed brown sugar**
¼ cup flour	**2 tablespoons milk or half-and-**
1 teaspoon cinnamon	**half**
¼ teaspoon salt	**½ cup chopped pecans**

Line a 9-inch pie plate with half the pastry.

Combine the sugar, flour, cinnamon and salt in a large bowl and mix well. Add the apples and toss to coat. Spoon into the pastry-lined pie plate. Dot with ¼ cup of the butter.

Top with the remaining pastry, sealing the edge and cutting vents. Bake at 425 degrees for 15 minutes.

Cover the pastry edge with strips of foil to prevent burning. Bake for 20 to 30 minutes or until golden brown. Remove from oven. Place on a baking sheet.

Melt the remaining ¼ cup butter in a saucepan. Stir in the brown sugar and milk. Bring to a boil. Remove from heat. Stir in the pecans.

Spoon the pecan mixture over the top of the pie. Bake for 2 to 3 minutes or until the topping is bubbly.

Cool for 1 hour or longer before serving.

Yield: 6 servings

Little White House Key Lime Pie

4 egg whites
¼ teaspoon cream of tartar
1½ cups sugar
4 egg yolks

3 to 4 tablespoons lime juice
2 teaspoons lime zest
1 cup whipping cream

Beat the egg whites with the cream of tartar in a mixer bowl until soft peaks form. Add 1 cup of the sugar gradually, beating until stiff peaks form. Spoon evenly into a greased 9-inch glass pie plate. Place in a cold oven. Bake at 250 degrees for 1 hour. Cool completely.

Beat the egg yolks in a mixer bowl until pale yellow. Add the remaining sugar, lime juice to taste and lime zest and mix well.

Pour into the top of a double boiler. Cook over hot water until thickened, stirring frequently. Cool the mixture.

Beat the whipping cream in a mixer bowl until stiff peaks form. Fold into the lime mixture. Spoon into the cooled shell. Refrigerate, covered, for 24 hours.

Variation: May substitute lemon juice and zest for the lime juice and zest.

Yield: 6 servings

Buttermilk Pie

½ cup butter
2 cups sugar
3 eggs
3 tablespoons flour

¼ teaspoon salt
1 cup buttermilk
1 unbaked (9-inch) pie shell
½ cup chopped pecans

Place the butter in a mixer bowl. Add the sugar ½ cup at a time, mixing well after each addition. Cream until light and fluffy. Add the eggs 1 at a time, mixing well after each addition.

Combine the flour and salt in a bowl and mix well. Add to the creamed mixture gradually, mixing well after each addition. Beat in the buttermilk. Pour into the pie shell.

Bake at 300 degrees for 1 hour. Sprinkle with the pecans. Bake for 30 minutes or until the pie is golden brown.

Yield: 6 servings

Wonderful Ice Cream Pie

18 vanilla wafers, crushed
½ gallon vanilla ice cream,
    softened
1 cup chopped Heath candy bar
1½ cups sugar

1 cup evaporated milk
¼ cup butter or margarine
¼ cup light corn syrup
⅛ teaspoon salt

Line the bottom and side of a 9-inch pie plate with the vanilla wafers.

Spoon half the ice cream over the wafers. Sprinkle with half the candy. Spoon the remaining ice cream over the candy. Freeze, covered, until firm.

Combine the sugar, evaporated milk, butter, corn syrup and salt in a saucepan. Bring to a boil. Boil over low heat for 1 minute, stirring constantly. Remove from heat. Stir in the remaining candy.

Cool, stirring occasionally. Serve the topping over slices of the pie.

Yield: 6 servings

Pecan Tart with Praline Cream

1 recipe (1-crust) pie pastry
3/4 cup sugar
3/4 cup light corn syrup
1/4 cup butter or margarine
3 eggs, lightly beaten

1 teaspoon vanilla extract
1/4 teaspoon salt
1 cup pecan halves
1/4 cup semisweet chocolate chips
Praline Cream

Roll the pie pastry into a 12-inch circle on a lightly floured surface. Fit into a 10-inch tart pan with removable bottom. Trim the edge. Prick the bottom and side with a fork. Bake at 450 degrees for 7 minutes.

Combine the sugar, corn syrup and butter in a saucepan. Cook over medium heat until the sugar dissolves and the butter melts, stirring constantly. Cool slightly.

Stir a small amount of the hot mixture into the beaten eggs in a bowl. Stir the eggs into the hot mixture. Add the vanilla and salt and mix well. Pour into the prepared pastry crust. Top with the pecan halves.

Bake at 325 degrees for 55 minutes or until set.

Place the chocolate chips in a sealable plastic bag. Submerge in hot water until the chocolate melts. Snip a tiny hole in the corner. Drizzle over the tart. Serve with Praline Cream.

Praline Cream

1 cup whipping cream
2 teaspoons praline liqueur

1 teaspoon vanilla extract
1/4 cup sifted confectioners' sugar

Combine the whipping cream, liqueur and vanilla in a mixer bowl. Beat at medium speed until foamy.

Add the confectioners' sugar 1 tablespoon at a time, mixing well after each addition. Beat until soft peaks form.

Yield: 8 servings

Fresh Lemon Tart

1 tart pastry
4 eggs
1 cup sugar
4 teaspoons grated lemon peel

½ cup fresh lemon juice
⅓ cup unsalted butter or
margarine

Roll the tart pastry into a 13-inch circle on a lightly floured surface. Fit into an 11-inch tart pan. Trim the edge. Prick the bottom and side with a fork. Bake at 400 degrees for 10 to 12 minutes or until golden brown. Cool on a wire rack.

Beat the eggs at high speed in a mixer bowl for 5 minutes or until the eggs are thick and pale yellow.

Add the sugar gradually, beating for 5 minutes or until the mixture doubles in size. Stir in the lemon peel and lemon juice. Pour into a large heavy saucepan.

Cook over medium heat for 5 to 10 minutes or until the mixture mounds and is fluffy, stirring constantly. Remove from heat.

Cut the butter into small pieces. Add to the filling. Stir until the butter is melted. Pour into the prepared pastry crust.

Bake at 400 degrees for 10 to 15 minutes or until golden. Cool on a wire rack. Serve plain or topped with whipped cream and fruit. Store, covered, in the refrigerator.

Yield: 12 servings

Campaign Cheesecake

1 cup graham cracker crumbs
½ cup finely chopped pecans
3 tablespoons sugar
1 teaspoon cinnamon
¼ cup melted margarine
2 (8-ounce) packages cream cheese, softened

½ cup sugar
2 eggs
½ teaspoon vanilla extract
⅓ cup sugar
4 cups thinly sliced peeled apples
¼ cup chopped pecans

Combine the graham cracker crumbs, ½ cup pecans, the 3 tablespoons sugar, ½ teaspoon of the cinnamon and margarine in a bowl and mix well. Press onto the bottom of a 9-inch springform pan. Bake in a preheated 350-degree oven for 10 minutes.

Cream the cream cheese and the ½ cup sugar in a mixer bowl until light and fluffy. Add the eggs 1 at a time, mixing well after each addition. Stir in the vanilla. Spoon into the prepared pan.

Combine ⅓ cup sugar and the remaining ½ teaspoon cinnamon in a bowl and mix well. Add the apples and toss to coat. Spoon over the cream cheese layer. Sprinkle with ¼ cup pecans.

Bake for 1 hour and 10 minutes. Loosen the cheesecake from the edge of the pan. Cool completely.

Store, covered, in the refrigerator.

Yield: 10 servings

Coco Mac Cheesecake

1²/₃ cups flaked coconut, toasted
½ cup ground pecans
2 tablespoons melted butter or
   margarine
3 (8-ounce) packages cream
   cheese, softened

½ cup sugar
1 teaspoon vanilla extract
¼ teaspoon almond extract
3 eggs
1 egg white
⅓ cup sugar

Combine 1 cup of the coconut, pecans and melted butter in a small bowl and mix well. Press into the bottom of a 9-inch springform pan.

Beat the cream cheese, ½ cup sugar, ½ teaspoon of the vanilla and almond extract at low speed in a mixer bowl until smooth.

Add the 3 eggs. Beat at low speed until blended; do not overbeat. Pour into the prepared pan. Place the pan on a baking sheet.

Bake at 350 degrees for 35 minutes. Remove from oven.

Beat the egg white and remaining ½ teaspoon of vanilla in a mixer bowl until soft peaks form. Add the sugar gradually, beating until stiff peaks form. Fold in the remaining ²/₃ cup coconut. Spread over the partially baked cheesecake.

Bake for 20 minutes; do not overbake. Remove the springform pan from the baking sheet. Cool the cheesecake on a wire rack for 15 minutes. Loosen the side of the cheesecake from the pan. Cool for 1 hour.

Chill, covered, for 4 hours or longer. Remove the side of the pan. Garnish with strawberries and additional toasted coconut.

Yield: 12 servings

First Lady Cheesecake

6 chocolate wafer cookies, finely
   crushed
1½ cups light cream cheese
1 cup sugar
1 cup low-fat cottage cheese
¼ cup plus 2 tablespoons baking
   cocoa

¼ cup flour
1 teaspoon vanilla extract
¼ teaspoon salt
¼ cup amaretto
1 egg
2 tablespoons miniature
   semisweet chocolate chips

Sprinkle the chocolate wafer crumbs in the bottom of a 7-inch springform pan.

Combine the cream cheese, sugar, cottage cheese, baking cocoa, flour, vanilla, salt and amaretto in a food processor container. Process until smooth. Add the egg and process until blended. Fold in the chocolate chips.

Pour the cream cheese mixture into the prepared pan. Bake at 300 degrees for 65 to 70 minutes or until the cheesecake is set. Place on a wire rack to cool completely.

Chill, covered, for 8 hours or longer.

Loosen the side of the cheesecake from the pan. Remove the side of the pan. Garnish with chocolate curls.

Variation: May substitute ¼ cup crème de menthe for the amaretto.

Yield: 10 servings

Praline Pecan Cheesecake

*1 (2-layer) package butter recipe
    cake mix*
*½ cup butter or margarine,
    softened*
*3 (8-ounce) packages cream
    cheese, softened*
½ cup sugar
3 tablespoons flour

1 to 1½ teaspoons rum extract
3 eggs
*4 (1-ounce) toffee candy bars,
    coarsely crushed*
½ cup packed brown sugar
1 cup chopped pecans
½ cup caramel ice cream topping

Combine the cake mix and butter in a large bowl. Beat at low speed until crumbly. Reserve 1 cup of the crumb mixture for topping. Press the remaining mixture onto the bottom and 1½ inches up the side of an ungreased 9- or 10-inch springform pan.

Combine the cream cheese, sugar, flour and rum extract in a bowl and beat until smooth. Add the eggs and mix well. Stir in the crushed candy. Pour into the prepared pan.

Combine the reserved crumb mixture, brown sugar and pecans and mix well. Sprinkle evenly over the cream cheese mixture.

Bake at 325 degrees for 70 minutes or until set and golden brown.

Drizzle caramel topping over the top. Bake for 8 to 10 minutes longer.

Cool for 30 minutes. Chill for 4 to 8 hours. Remove side of pan.

Yield: 10 servings

★ ★ ★ ★ ★

"After-Dinner-Mint" Fruit

½ pint strawberries
½ pint raspberries
½ pint blackberries
½ pint blueberries

2 tablespoons brown sugar
1 tablespoon Triple Sec
1½ cups sour cream

Wash the strawberries and remove the stems. Cut into ¼-inch pieces. Place in a large bowl.

Wash the raspberries, blackberries and blueberries. Pat dry. Combine with the strawberries.

Combine the brown sugar and Triple Sec in a bowl. Stir until the brown sugar is dissolved. Add the sour cream and mix well. Pour over the berries and stir until the berries are coated.

Spoon into 6 large wine glasses. Garnish each with a mint leaf.

Yield: 6 servings

Caramelized Bananas

¼ cup packed light brown sugar
¼ teaspoon ground cinnamon
4 small bananas

1 pint vanilla or favorite ice
**   cream**

Preheat the broiler. Line a broiler pan, with rack removed, with foil. Grease the foil.

Combine the brown sugar and cinnamon in a bowl and mix well.

Slice the bananas diagonally ¾ inch thick. Place in the prepared pan. Sprinkle with the brown sugar mixture. Broil 5 to 7 inches from the heat source for 2 to 3 minutes or until the sugar is melted and caramelized.

Scoop the ice cream into dessert bowls. Spoon the banana mixture over the ice cream.

Yield: 4 servings

Broiled Coconut Pineapple

6 tablespoons melted butter
16 thin slices peeled fresh
**   pineapple**

6 tablespoons brown sugar
6 tablespoons flaked sweetened
**   coconut**

Preheat the broiler. Brush a little of the butter on the bottom of a shallow oblong baking dish.

Arrange the pineapple slices, slightly overlapping, in the prepared baking dish. Sprinkle with the brown sugar. Drizzle with the remaining butter.

Broil 4 inches from the heat source for 2 to 3 minutes or until the top is golden brown and bubbly.

Sprinkle with the coconut. Broil for 1 minute or until the coconut is toasted.

Yield: 8 servings

Chilled Strawberry Soup with Pound Cake Croutons

4 cups sliced fresh strawberries
1 banana, quartered
1 cup sour cream

1 cup pineapple or orange juice
1½ cups ½-inch cubes of
**   pound cake**

Combine the strawberries, banana, sour cream and juice in a blender container and process until well blended.

Preheat broiler. Arrange the cake cubes in a single layer on a baking sheet. Broil until lightly browned on all sides, turning occasionally.

Ladle the soup into 6 bowls. Top with the croutons.

Yield: 6 servings

Ice Cream Torte

1 cup vanilla wafer crumbs
¼ cup finely chopped almonds
3 tablespoons melted butter
**1 (4-ounce) package vanilla
   instant pudding mix**

1 cup milk
½ teaspoon almond extract
½ cup whipping cream, whipped
**½ gallon chocolate ice cream,
   softened**

Combine the vanilla wafer crumbs, almonds and butter in a bowl and mix well. Press onto the bottom of a 9-inch springform pan. Freeze until firm.

Beat the pudding mix and milk at low speed in a mixer bowl for 1 minute. Fold in the almond extract and whipped cream.

Spoon a thin layer of ice cream over the pressed crumbs. Layer the pudding and remaining ice cream half at a time alternately over the ice cream layer.

Freeze, covered, for 8 to 12 hours. Garnish with cherries and additional whipped cream.

Yield: 12 servings

Peach Cardinale

4 peaches
3 cups water
1 cup sugar
1 tablespoon vanilla extract
1 (10-ounce) package frozen
    raspberries, thawed

1 tablespoon sugar
2 teaspoons cornstarch
¼ cup water
½ cup whipping cream,
    whipped

Bring enough water to cover the peaches to a boil in a saucepan. Blanch the peaches in the boiling water for 20 seconds. Remove with a slotted spoon and plunge into ice water. Peel the peaches. Cut the peaches into halves.

Combine the 3 cups water and 1 cup sugar in a Dutch oven. Bring to a boil. Cook for 3 minutes, stirring occasionally. Reduce the heat to low. Stir in the vanilla. Add the peach halves. Simmer, uncovered, for 10 to 15 minutes or until the peaches are tender. Chill, covered, for 1 hour or up to 2 days.

Press the raspberries through a sieve. Discard the seeds.

Combine the 1 tablespoon sugar and the cornstarch in a saucepan and mix well. Stir in the ¼ cup water. Stir in the raspberry purée. Bring to a boil over medium heat, stirring constantly. Boil for 1 minute, stirring constantly. Chill, covered, until cooled completely.

Spoon the whipped cream into 4 individual dessert dishes. Place 2 peach halves together over the whipped cream. Spoon ¼ of the sauce around each peach. Garnish with mint leaves.

Yield: 4 servings

Sweet Peaches with Creamy Zabaglione

8 medium peaches
¼ cup orange liqueur
¼ cup plus 3 tablespoons sugar
3 egg yolks
⅓ cup marsala

1 cup whipping cream
1 tablespoon confectioners' sugar
8 amaretti cookie halves,
    crumbled

Bring enough water to cover the peaches to a boil in a saucepan. Blanch the peaches in the boiling water for 20 seconds. Remove with a slotted spoon and plunge into ice water. Peel the peaches. Cut the peaches into halves. Cut the halves into slices ¼ inch thick.

Combine the orange liqueur and ¼ cup of the sugar in a bowl and mix well. Add the peaches and toss to coat. Chill for 2 to 5 hours.

Whisk the egg yolks with the remaining 3 tablespoons sugar in a small bowl for 2 minutes or until thick and pale yellow. Whisk in the marsala.

Place the small bowl over a saucepan of simmering water. Cook over low heat for 8 minutes or until very pale and of the desired consistency, whisking constantly. Place the bowl in a large bowl of ice water to cool.

Whip the cream and confectioners' sugar in a mixer bowl until soft peaks form. Fold in the cooled zabaglione.

Divide the peach mixture among 8 dessert dishes. Spoon a generous dollop of the zabaglione over the peaches. Sprinkle with the amaretti.

Yield: 8 servings

Cappuccino Cream

1 cup strong coffee, room
   temperature
½ cup milk
8 ounces cream cheese, softened
1 (4-ounce) package vanilla
   instant pudding mix

¼ teaspoon cinnamon
1 (8-ounce) container whipped
   topping

Combine the coffee and milk in a bowl and mix well. Place the cream cheese in a mixer bowl. Add the coffee mixture to the cream cheese gradually, beating at medium speed until smooth.

Add the pudding mix and cinnamon. Beat at low speed for 1 minute. Fold in 2 cups of the whipped topping.

Spoon the mixture into 6 dessert glasses or a 1-quart serving bowl. Chill until ready to serve.

Top with the remaining whipped topping. Garnish with chocolate-covered coffee beans and fresh mint. Sprinkle with additional cinnamon.

Yield: 6 servings

Ozark Pudding

1 egg	*¼ teaspoon baking powder*
¾ cup sugar	*⅛ teaspoon salt*
1 teaspoon vanilla extract	*½ cup chopped apples*
2 tablespoons flour	*½ cup chopped walnuts*

Combine the egg and sugar in a mixer bowl. Beat until smooth. Add the vanilla and mix well.

Sift the flour, baking powder and salt into a bowl. Add to the sugar mixture and mix well. Stir in the apples and walnuts. Spoon into a greased 8-inch-square baking pan. Bake at 350 degrees for 35 minutes.

Yield: 9 servings

"In reading the lives of great men, I found that the first
victory they won was over themselves and their carnal urges.
Self-discipline with all of them came first."

Food Guide Pyramid

A Guide to Daily Food Choices

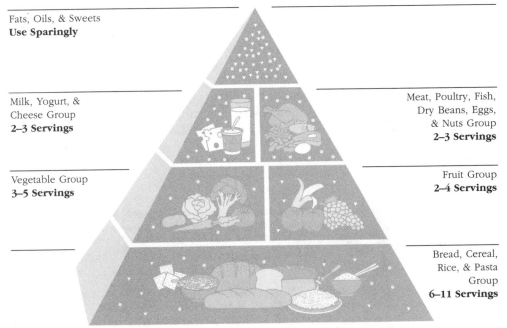

Fats, Oils, & Sweets
Use Sparingly

Milk, Yogurt, &
Cheese Group
2–3 Servings

Meat, Poultry, Fish,
Dry Beans, Eggs,
& Nuts Group
2–3 Servings

Vegetable Group
3–5 Servings

Fruit Group
2–4 Servings

Bread, Cereal,
Rice, & Pasta
Group
6–11 Servings

Source: U.S. Department of Agriculture and the U.S. Department of Health and Human Services.

Key

● Fat (naturally occurring and added)

▼ Sugars (added)

These symbols show fat and added sugars in foods. They come mostly
from the fats, oils, and sweets group. But foods in other groups—such
as cheese or ice cream from the milk group or French fries from the
vegetable group—can also provide fat and added sugars.

Looking at the Pieces of the Pyramid

The Food Guide Pyramid emphasizes foods from the five major food groups shown in the
three lower sections of the Pyramid. Each of these food groups provides some, but not all, of
the nutrients you need. Foods in one group cannot replace those in another. No one of these
major food groups is more important than another—for good health, you need them all.

Nutritional Profile Guidelines

The editors have attempted to present these family recipes in a format that allows approximate nutritional values to be computed. Persons with dietary or health problems or whose diets require close monitoring should not rely solely on the nutritional information provided. They should consult their physicians or a registered dietitian for specific information.

Abbreviations

Cal — Calories	T Fat — Total Fat	Sod — Sodium
Prot — Protein	Chol — Cholesterol	g — gram
Carbo — Carbohydrates	Fiber — Dietary Fiber	mg — milligram

Nutritional information for these recipes is computed from information derived from many sources, including materials supplied by the United States Department of Agriculture, computer databanks, and journals in which the information is assumed to be in the public domain. However, many specialty items, new products, and processed foods may not be available from these sources or may vary from the average values used in these profiles. More information on new and/or specific products may be obtained by reading the nutrient labels. Unless otherwise specified, the nutritional profile of these recipes is based on all measurements being level.

- Artificial sweeteners vary in use and strength so should be used "to taste," using the recipe ingredients as a guideline. Sweeteners using aspartame (NutraSweet and Equal) should not be used as a sweetener in recipes involving prolonged heating, which reduces the sweet taste. For further information on the use of these sweeteners, refer to the package.
- Alcoholic ingredients have been analyzed for the basic information. Cooking causes the evaporation of alcohol, which decreases alcoholic and caloric content.
- Buttermilk, sour cream, and yogurt are the types available commercially.
- Cake mixes that are prepared using package directions include 3 eggs and ½ cup oil.
- Chicken, cooked for boning and chopping, has been roasted; this method yields the lowest caloric values.
- Cottage cheese is cream-style with 4.2% creaming mixture. Dry-curd cottage cheese has no creaming mixture.
- Eggs are all large. To avoid raw eggs that may carry salmonella, as in eggnog or 6-week muffin batter, use an equivalent amount of commercial egg substitute.
- Flour is unsifted all-purpose flour.
- Garnishes, serving suggestions, and other optional information and variations are not included in the profile.
- Margarine and butter are regular, not whipped or presoftened.
- Milk is whole milk, 3.5% butterfat. Low-fat milk is 1% butterfat. Evaporated milk is whole milk with 60% of the water removed.
- Oil is vegetable cooking oil. Shortening is hydrogenated vegetable shortening.
- Salt and other ingredients to taste, as noted in the ingredients, have not been included in the nutritional profile.
- If a choice of ingredients has been given, the profile reflects the first option. If a choice of amounts has been given, the profile reflects the greater amount.

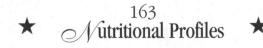

Pg #	Recipe Title (Approx Per Serving)	Cal	Prot (g)	Carbo (g)	T Fat (g)	% Fat Cal	Chol (mg)	Fiber (g)	Sod (mg)
9	What a Ball	177	4	6	16	78	26	1	200
9	Sunflower Cheese Ball	378	10	26	28	64	28	3	607
10	Smoky Salmon Ball	111	9	1	9	66	36	<1	141
10	Great Balls of Shrimp	111	6	7	7	56	49	<1	161
11	Baked Goat Cheese	269	14	9	21	68	45	2	368
11	Country Fare	306	8	1	30	88	45	<1	352
12	Double-Up Black Bean Dip	37	2	5	1	26	2	2	146
13	Black Bean Salsa	96	2	11	5	48	0	3	248
13	Gemini Crab Meat Dip	115	3	1	10	82	33	<1	113
14	Island Salsa	38	1	10	<1	4	0	1	294
14	Jackson County Caviar	45	1	4	4	65	0	1	419
15	Loaded Spinach Dip	175	8	4	14	72	37	1	417
15	Reuben Dip	122	7	1	10	72	35	<1	238
16	Toasted Almond Party Spread	190	7	4	17	78	42	<1	165
17	Gouda Cheese Bundles	204	9	12	13	59	55	<1	522
17	Wrapped Asparagus	387	24	6	30	70	57	1	1737
18	Crescent Veggie Appetizers	174	3	13	12	62	19	1	265
19	Whistle Stop Wings*	173	13	19	5	24	29	1	690
20	Amaretto Lemon Freeze	111	<1	22	<1	1	0	<1	9
20	Cappuccino Mix	115	1	26	2	16	0	1	45
21	Best-Kept-Secret Margaritas	389	<1	47	<1	0	0	1	<1
21	Frozen Margaritas	127	<1	18	<1	0	0	<1	1
22	Peach Fuzz	70	<1	10	<1	0	0	1	<1
22	Piña Colada Slush	106	<1	17	2	16	0	<1	9
25	Cream of Brie and Red Pepper Soup	599	22	11	53	78	184	2	1294
26	Cheesy Clam Chowder	192	6	14	13	61	40	2	934
26	First Edition Lentil Soup	336	20	43	10	27	22	13	542
27	Gazpacho	311	4	22	25	69	0	5	313
28	Lasagna Soup	492	27	47	21	39	61	3	887
29	Pot of Gold Soup	357	4	23	29	71	98	4	979
29	Three Trails Cheese Soup	541	18	23	42	69	84	2	1289
30	ABC Sandwiches	457	22	37	24	48	54	3	902
30	Grilled Bacon Sandwiches	571	27	30	38	60	99	2	877
31	MJC Croissant Sandwiches	676	29	47	41	55	127	4	1773
32	Sweet Smoky Sandwiches	354	22	38	13	32	58	3	1217
33	Chocolate Zucchini Bread	221	3	28	12	46	27	1	313
34	Brookside Stromboli	650	29	40	43	58	153	2	1451
35	Dilly Bread	212	8	31	6	26	37	1	437
36	Orange Cranberry Bread	205	4	36	6	24	18	1	198
37	Sunrise Muffins	192	6	31	6	25	33	1	353
38	Blanketed Grapefruit Wedges	304	3	43	15	42	52	1	79
39	Frosty Fruit Cup	104	1	27	<1	1	0	1	2
39	Cranberry Coffee Cake	349	4	37	19	48	68	2	340
40	Holiday Brunch Cake	677	5	78	40	52	84	2	378
41	Philly Brunch Cake	264	4	32	14	47	62	<1	293
42	Overnight French Toast	327	11	42	13	35	181	2	619
42	Brunch Pizza	145	8	12	7	46	140	1	125

Pg #	Recipe Title (Approx Per Serving)	Cal	Prot (g)	Carbo (g)	T Fat (g)	% Fat Cal	Chol (mg)	Fiber (g)	Sod (mg)
45	Woodland Salad	159	7	7	13	67	6	3	807
46	White Bean Salad	533	11	22	46	76	17	5	231
46	Broccoli Cashew Salad	446	10	15	39	78	37	2	467
47	Off the Cob Salad	244	6	32	13	44	0	5	29
48	Shoepeg Salad	141	2	15	8	51	7	3	108
48	Wild Craisin Corn Salad	239	7	37	8	30	0	4	541
49	New New Potato Salad	193	5	27	8	36	13	3	531
49	Red and Bleu Potato Salad	292	8	32	15	44	18	3	634
50	Herby Tomato Salad	200	2	9	18	78	0	2	14
51	Spinach Salad with Strawberries	451	7	26	37	71	13	3	271
52	Spinach Salad with Pears	173	3	13	13	64	0	4	61
52	Blue Ridge Salad	358	12	6	32	80	181	3	584
53	Crysler Coleslaw	407	3	18	37	80	27	4	320
53	Kraut Melange	331	1	61	12	31	0	3	886
54	Artichoke Rice Salad	883	10	60	67	68	53	6	1373
55	Cashew Wild Rice Salad	421	15	39	23	50	27	2	709
56	Herbed Orzo Salad	281	8	43	8	26	0	2	77
56	Shrimp and Couscous Salad	351	29	28	12	33	231	3	625
57	Lemony Couscous Salad	281	8	41	10	30	0	4	102
57	Couscous Alfresco	317	13	39	13	35	25	4	372
58	Southwest Confetti Salad	541	8	36	42	68	0	4	276
59	Cropaico Salad	315	9	23	21	59	16	4	901
60	Fruity Chicken Salad	625	24	29	46	66	92	4	517
61	Wildly Delicious Turkey Salad	299	19	28	12	35	35	3	797
62	Ham & Asparagus Tortellini Salad	367	18	40	14	35	41	3	624
65	Beef and Bean Burritos	589	39	59	21	33	80	6	1279
66	Quick Cassoulet	202	15	12	10	43	40	3	265
67	Mediterranean Veal Sauté	475	44	16	23	44	181	3	1194
68	Pork Loin and Kraut	380	49	5	17	41	138	4	909
68	Sesame Grilled Pork Tenderloin	238	26	9	10	40	67	1	930
69	Mapled Pork Chops	171	20	10	5	27	51	<1	461
69	Pork Chops with Brandy Sauce	375	21	18	23	55	107	2	53
70	Honey-Chili Grilled Pork Chops	375	34	37	11	26	86	2	476
71	Peach Fritters*	399	12	77	4	10	110	4	508
72	Rack of Lamb	406	40	14	20	46	119	<1	324
73	Broiled Lamb Chops	230	28	<1	12	50	87	<1	77
74	Blowin' Smoke Chicken Stix	316	55	5	7	21	150	1	214
75	Chicken and Lemon Cream	965	63	66	48	46	263	1	1441
76	Chicken Breasts with Angel Hair	936	65	43	53	52	170	1	1086
76	Backyard Marinade	148	4	7	11	68	0	<1	3509
77	Chutney Chicken	419	28	6	31	68	106	<1	248
77	Clubhouse Chicken	266	21	5	18	61	84	1	770
78	Chicken Spiedini	690	37	17	53	69	88	1	599
79	Comfort Chicken	827	61	67	34	37	170	6	1584
80	Honey Basil Chicken	341	55	12	7	18	146	<1	928
81	Hot Chicken	600	13	24	50	75	63	5	1030
81	Garlic Marinade	340	4	2	36	93	8	<1	419
82	Knoepker's Creamed Chicken	1097	38	45	86	70	275	3	1765

Pg #	Recipe Title (Approx Per Serving)	Cal	Prot (g)	Carbo (g)	T Fat (g)	% Fat Cal	Chol (mg)	Fiber (g)	Sod (mg)
83	Piggyback Chicken Fingers	265	35	16	6	20	86	<1	292
84	Summer Lime Chicken Breast	493	55	12	24	45	146	1	422
85	Stir-Fry Broccoli	97	4	7	7	61	0	3	151
85	R & B Chicken	587	56	73	7	11	110	13	2083
86	Pasta Dijon Au Artichokes	806	58	85	26	29	106	6	673
87	Roasted Cornish Hens	691	62	7	45	60	188	<1	2427
88	Midway Stew	443	29	79	7	12	46	15	2294
89	Roasted Salmon and Vegetables	345	33	8	18	49	102	2	155
90	Succulent Salmon	851	56	8	65	69	213	1	655
91	Clam Tetrazzini	662	26	56	38	51	157	3	757
92	Saul's Flaming Swordfish	344	27	6	19	50	53	1	124
92	Scallops au Gratin	224	10	9	17	66	63	1	405
93	Sausalito Scallops	436	25	43	17	35	28	3	690
94	Scallops, Zucchini and Tomatoes over Penne	581	24	88	15	23	18	5	394
95	Pasta with Shrimp and Feta	850	40	134	16	17	144	8	902
96	Shrimp Pizza	959	65	70	47	44	388	2	2014
96	Shrimp Creole	283	24	40	3	10	164	5	558
97	Smith's Shrimp Sauté	398	12	34	20	45	92	1	136
98	Amer's Red Hot Pasta	866	16	94	47	49	0	4	325
99	Lemon Pasta	547	19	71	22	35	25	3	869
99	Egg Noodles & Poppy Seed Sauce	749	25	97	26	31	122	6	369
100	Legislative Lasagna	414	28	20	24	53	112	2	719
101	Linguine with Two Sauces	347	17	55	5	14	12	5	462
102	Pasta with Tomatoes, Mozzarella	603	23	72	24	37	44	3	226
102	Pasta Baked with Stilton & Port	318	11	39	11	30	22	1	220
103	Pasta Vegetable Ragout	469	12	72	15	29	0	6	18
104	Star Spangled Pasta	869	26	95	43	44	38	4	827
104	Fresh Vegetable Linguine	338	10	30	21	54	59	3	380
107	Green Vegetable Medley	88	5	12	3	31	8	5	653
108	Bleu Cheese Green Beans	267	8	9	23	75	21	4	485
109	Green Bean Pepper Parmesan	89	5	7	5	47	7	3	257
110	Sweet and Sour Beans	127	3	16	6	42	16	4	278
110	Tangy Green Beans	191	6	9	16	71	32	3	274
111	Hawaiian Vegetables	106	1	23	2	13	0	3	193
112	Baked Chile-Cheese Corn	311	11	25	20	56	61	4	462
112	Golden Potatoes	262	7	27	15	49	43	2	337
113	Dijon Potatoes**	139	4	24	3	19	8	2	55
114	Potato Gratin	315	9	19	23	65	81	2	186
115	Swiss Potato Gratin	470	13	49	23	43	80	4	105
116	Ratatouille	156	3	17	10	51	0	5	791
117	Roasted Roots	221	3	34	9	35	0	6	510
118	Red Tape Rhubarb	347	3	49	17	42	41	3	265
118	Hearty Sweet Potatoes	668	6	81	38	50	133	4	277
119	Summer Tomato Basil Tart	527	23	37	32	55	142	10	1068
120	Vegetable Frittata	461	21	27	31	59	228	3	956
121	Zorba's Zucchini	251	11	16	17	59	51	3	913
122	Herb Butters	103	<1	<1	12	98	31	<1	118

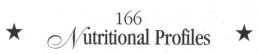

Pg #	Recipe Title (Approx Per Serving)	Cal	Prot (g)	Carbo (g)	T Fat (g)	% Fat Cal	Chol (mg)	Fiber (g)	Sod (mg)
122	Herbed Caper Butter	102	<1	<1	12	99	31	<1	160
123	Red Wine Butter for Steak	177	<1	2	14	72	39	<1	150
123	Portobello Mushroom Sauce	221	3	7	18	70	0	3	302
124	Sweet and Spicy Couscous	419	12	78	8	17	0	6	305
125	Baked Grits	380	13	16	29	69	134	<1	636
126	Orzo and Rice Pilaf	230	8	38	4	17	1	1	657
126	DBS Wild Rice	419	15	41	22	46	31	4	1283
129	Harry T's Apple Cake	468	4	73	19	36	48	1	259
130	Wacky Chocolate Cake	140	2	23	5	30	0	1	123
130	Very Best Homemade Ice Cream	277	5	26	17	56	105	0	132
131	Black Pepper Pound Cake	316	3	32	19	55	103	<1	235
132	Butternut Pound Cake	577	6	73	30	46	131	1	222
133	Hershey's Pound Cake	784	10	103	40	44	104	4	304
134	Chocolate Praline Cake	512	6	46	35	60	100	1	387
135	Pumpkin Gingerbread	682	6	86	37	47	107	2	509
136	Whiskey Fudge Cake	393	5	43	21	48	103	3	245
137	Apple Surprise Cupcakes	268	3	32	15	49	37	1	240
138	Bess' Signature Coconut Balls	75	1	10	4	43	4	<1	51
139	Spice Cookies with Pumpkin Dip	369	4	55	15	37	59	2	505
140	Coffee Iced Oatmeal Cookies	289	3	41	13	41	25	1	228
141	Pecan Tea Cookies	205	2	18	15	63	28	1	139
141	Disappearing Brownie Cookies	275	3	39	14	43	24	2	99
142	Choco-Sticks	126	1	15	8	52	28	1	56
143	Oh Susannah Bars	430	4	57	22	44	72	1	336
143	Red Raspberry and White Bars	496	7	62	25	45	91	1	226
144	Tailgate Brownies	277	3	24	20	63	35	1	100
145	Show Me More Brownies	587	9	86	25	37	75	4	514
146	Better Than Apple Pie	758	3	93	43	50	62	3	637
147	Little White House Key Lime Pie	385	5	53	18	41	196	<1	57
148	Buttermilk Pie	686	8	88	35	45	149	1	491
148	Wonderful Ice Cream Pie	898	10	129	40	39	119	1	431
149	Pecan Tart with Praline Cream	593	6	64	37	54	136	1	326
150	Fresh Lemon Tart	237	3	27	13	50	85	1	144
151	Campaign Cheesecake	428	6	39	29	59	92	2	273
152	Coco Mac Cheesecake	364	7	21	29	70	121	1	234
153	First Lady Cheesecake	254	9	34	9	30	41	1	358
154	Praline Pecan Cheesecake	820	11	86	50	54	169	2	726
155	"After-Dinner-Mint" Fruit	192	2	19	12	56	26	4	34
155	Caramelized Bananas	266	3	50	8	25	29	2	59
156	Broiled Coconut Pineapple	197	1	28	10	44	23	1	113
156	Chilled Strawberry Soup	212	3	27	11	46	48	3	79
157	Ice Cream Torte	510	8	47	32	57	184	<1	251
158	Peach Cardinale	437	2	85	11	23	41	5	13
159	Sweet Peaches***	238	2	27	13	47	121	2	16
160	Cappuccino Cream	324	4	27	21	61	44	0	360
161	Ozark Pudding	126	2	20	5	32	24	1	54

Nutritional profile does not include *oil for deep frying, **salt-free Dijon mustard, ***amaretti cookies.

 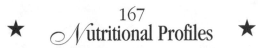

★　　★　　★　　★　　★

ACKNOWLEDGMENTS

"*If* You Can't Stand the Heat, Get Out of the Kitchen!"
VOLUME II

Special thanks to

Pauline Testerman of the Truman Library Archives

Dr. Benjamin Zobrist, retired
Director of the Truman Library and Museum

The Harry S. Truman Library and Museum

The Independence School District

Dan Barbour for photography of the Truman Library &
Museum found on inside front and back covers

Dena Morrison, League President 1998-1999,
for historical text on section dividers

*All photos courtesy of the National Park Service
and the Harry S. Truman Library Archives
unless otherwise credited.*

★　　★　　★　　★　　★

★ ★ ★ ★ ★

CONTRIBUTORS

This cookbook was produced in the grand spirit of the women of the Independence Junior Service League; women inspired by dedication, devotion, and perseverance to accomplish goals and projects for the benefit of the community.

All proceeds from the sale of this cookbook will be returned to the Eastern Jackson County community through the Community Trust Fund.

Kristie Agee
Judy Austin
Jo Ann Axtell
Wendy Biggerstaff
Mary Catherine Blank
Diana Blessen
Kim Buckley
Betty Bundschu
Amy Barbour Burnett
Sandy Burry
Vicki Campbell
Kyle Carson
Maureen Champion
Melodie Chrisman
Helen Coil
Roberta "Poo" Coker
Cheryl Comer
Meghan Conger
Larna Constance
Susan Crowley
Michele Crumbaugh
Carol Draveling
Becky Elrod
Jill Esry

Nancy Esry
Susan Evans
Lana Farnsworth
Judy Forrester
Colleen Foudree
Myla Gentry
Sue Gentry
Janet Gibbs
Lori Grubb
Jacqueline Hahn
Beth Hammer
Lisa Hammett
Diane Hawkins
Joy Hobick
Shirley Holder
Judy Johnson
Shellie Page Kemna
Beth Legler
Jane Leonard
Oraleen Manthe
Liz McClure
Arlene Miller
Virginia Miller
Claudia Moore

Dena Morrison
Lois Morrison
Mary Nesselrode
Cindy Petrie
Sandra Plumlee-
    Hermans
Patricia Shelton
Sharon Shook
Kim Shultz
Patti Simcosky
Gloria Smith
Vici Stumpenhaus
Jane Taylor
Carol Thompson
Barbara Thornton
Toni Thornton
Christine Walker
Joan Walker
Jayme Watkins
Judy Weatherford
Janet Wheeler
Lori Withers
Lennie Wyre

★ ★ ★ ★ ★

Index

★　★　★　★　★

ORDER INFORMATION

"*If* You Can't Stand the Heat, Get Out of the Kitchen!"
VOLUME II

Cookbook Merchandising
c/o The Independence Junior Service League
P.O. Box 1571
Independence, MO 64055

Please send _____ copies of *"Can't Stand the Heat, Vol. II"*, at $18.95 plus $3.00 (shipping and handling) per book.

Enclosed is my check for $_____,
made payable to Independence JSL.

Ship to:
Name _____
Address _____
City, State and Zip Code_____

Please send _____ copies of *The Bess Collection*, at $18.95 plus $3.00 (shipping and handling) per book.

Enclosed is my check for $_____,
made payable to Independence JSL.

Ship to:
Name _____
Address _____
City, State and Zip Code_____

★　★　★　★　★